# POWER REAL ESTATE LETTERS

## A PROFESSIONAL'S RESOURCE FOR SUCCESS

## William H. Pivar
## Corinne E. Pivar

Real Estate
Education Company
a division of Dearborn Financial Publishing, Inc.

While a great deal of care has been taken to provide accurate and current information, the ideas, suggestions, general principles and conclusions presented in this text are subject to local, state and federal laws and regulations, court cases and any revisions of same. The reader thus is urged to consult legal counsel regarding any points of law—this publication should not be used as a substitute for competent legal advice.

Publisher: Kathleen A. Welton
Acquisitions Editor: Wendy Lochner
Project Editor: Jack L. Kiburz
Cover Design: Sam Concialdi

©1990 by Dearborn Financial Publishing, Inc.
Published by Real Estate Education Company,
a division of Dearborn Financial Publishing, Inc.

Printed in the United States of America.

91 92 10 9 8 7 6 5 4

**Library of Congress Cataloging-in-Publication Data**

Pivar, William H.
    Power real estate letters: a professional resource for success /
    by William H. Pivar and Corinne E. Pivar.
    p. cm.
    ISBN 0-88462-974-0
    1. Real estate business—Records and correspondence.  I. Pivar,
    Corinne E.  II. Title.
HD1386.5.P58   1990
651.7'5—dc20                                              89-24067
                                                             CIP

# CONTENTS

# INTRODUCTION

In terms of communications effectiveness, personal contact usually ranks first, with telephone conversations coming in second. This leaves letters in third place. Letters do, however, have some distinct advantages over other methods of communications. Besides providing a written record of the communication, in which there is little room to question the message conveyed, letters provide a clarity of intent often lost in verbal communication. There are also times when letters are the only feasible way to communicate effectively because of the recipient's inaccessibility, the sheer volume of persons to be contacted, or the complexity of the information to be conveyed.

In this book, we have provided letters for situations in which personal contact is often the desired method, such as when presenting offers or requesting price reduction, and when dealing with personnel problems. When considering each situation, ask yourself what method of communication is best. If a letter is not the best method, use the better method unless it is not feasible.

The most important attribute of any business letter is clarity. It must convey to the reader the writer's message in an unambiguous manner. One of the keys to achieving clarity is brevity. For this reason, the letters in this book are generally very short and to the point. Short letters are more likely to be fully read and understood by the reader.

In terms of mailing volume, most real estate letters are those soliciting listings of buyers. We have therefore included a number of these "fliers" in this book. Even though they may not be in letter format, they are nevertheless letters in the sense that they are written communications essential to real estate business, and conveyed through the mail.

These samples will fit over 90 percent of average real estate office's letter-writing needs. (Material that is optional or that you can personalize is italicized and placed in brackets to help to customize your letters.)

The letters in this book are presented in "block" style, just one of several styles that could have been used. (We have left blank the areas for the recipient's name, address and the signature, which should appear aligned with the left margin.) While we prefer this format, others prefer indented paragraphs and centered signatures. We do not feel the format is a significant factor in communication; if you feel more comfortable with another format, then please use it.

When you use this book to produce letters, consider using your word processor or computer to compose them. You can then set up and number files for letters stored in the computer. A new letter can then be quickly prepared through minor alterations to your sample letter in storage.

If you think there is a need for letters that are not included in this book, please let us know so we can add them in later editions. You may contact us at 75-496 Desert Park Drive, Indian Wells, CA 92210-8356.

# Chapter

# 1

# Letting People Know You Are a Real Estate Agent

# Letter to Friend or Acquaintance on Joining Firm #1

[*Date*]

_____

_____

_____

Guess what, _____ :

I am now a sales associate with [*Clyde Realty*]. I have completed a course of study for the state examination as well as the [*Clyde Realty*] training program. I am now ready, willing and able to help you meet your present and future real estate needs as a buyer, seller, renter or landlord.

Besides wanting to be your personal real estate agent, I would certainly appreciate hearing from you if you know of anyone contemplating a purchase or sale.

Your friend,

_____

**NOTE:** *You could add a handwritten note to the bottom asking about family members by name, in order to personalize the letter. You might also want to indicate that you will be phoning your friend by noting, "I will be calling you in a few days to discuss your present or future real estate needs." This forces the recipient to give thought to his or her real estate needs.*

*See the notes following the next letter as to enclosing your card.*

# Letter to Friend or Acquaintance on Joining Firm #2

[*Date*]

_____

_____

_____

Dear _____ :

I have recently joined the real estate firm of [*Clyde Realty*] as a [*sales associate*]. After many weeks of study and training, I am now prepared to meet the needs of all my friends and neighbors.

If you or any of our friends and neighbors have real estate needs as either potential buyers or sellers, I hope you will think of me. I have enclosed one of my new cards.

Yours truly,

_____

**NOTE:** *This letter is written for a new licensee. It will be especially effective if the card includes your picture so the reader can identify you with your letter. Besides your personal friends and neighbors, the letter should go to people you do business with, close friends of family members, parents of your children's friends, members of organizations you belong to including your church, and so on.*

*Consider adding "I will be calling in a few days to discuss your present or future real estate needs."*

# Broker Letter to Neighbors
# of New Salesperson

[*Date*]

_____

_____

_____

Dear _____ :

[*Judith Reilly*], your neighbor who lives at [*111 Midvale Lane*], has recently joined our firm as [*a sales associate*] [*an associate broker*]. [*Judith*] has been your neighbor for [*four*] years. [*She*] and [*her husband*] have [*two children, Lisa age nine and Jeffrey age seven, both of whom attend Midvale School. Judith is a graduate of Ohio State and previously worked in marketing*]. [*She*] has just completed our training program and will be specializing in [*residential sales*] in [*Orchard Ridge*]. If you or any of your friends have any real estate needs, we hope you will contact [*Judith*]. I have enclosed one of her new cards.

Sincerely,


_____


**NOTE:** *This letter should paint the employee as a person the reader will want to know. It should be mailed over a several block radius of the new employee's home as well as to the employee's special friends and, if the employee has children, to the parents of their friends. The employee's picture should be on the card enclosed so neighbors who have seen him or her can relate to the employee.*

# Notice to Friends, Acquaintances, Past Customers and Clients When You Change Offices

[*Date*]

_____

_____

_____

Dear _____ :

Just a note to let you know I am at a new address. I am now a [*sales associate*] [*associate broker*] with [*Clyde Realty*] at their office [*on Bellflower Blvd*]. I really like this office, as we have a group of energetic professionals who work together as a team to meet both buyer and seller needs.

If there is any way I can help you in meeting your real estate needs, don't hesitate to let me know. I have enclosed one of my new cards.

Yours truly,

_____

**NOTE:** *If the card or letter has your photo on it, the effectiveness of the letter will be greatly enhanced, as the reader can then place your face with your name.*

*Mail this letter to friends, neighbors, acquaintances and service people you do business with; members of organizations you belong to including your church; friends of family members; the parents of your children's friends; previous buyers and sellers you have had dealings with; and your active files of prospective buyers and sellers.*

# Chapter

# 2

# Listing Solicitation Letters—General

# Want to Know the Value #1

### Rumpelstiltskin

could turn straw into gold. We have a proven track record of performing the same feat with real estate.

Let me show you what a sale of your property could mean in terms of actual cash in your hands. Call today, and I will prepare a computerized competitive market analysis that will reveal how much cash is actually trapped within your property.

**NOTE:** *A better approach might be to replace the last sentence with: "I will be calling you within the next few days to discuss how we will determine the amount of cash actually trapped within your property." This forces the recipient to give consideration to the thought of a sale.*

*You might want to consider enclosing the Free Market Analysis Certificate, page 19, with this flier.*

# Want to Know the Value #2

## How Much Money Is Locked up in Your Home?

Because of high demand in [*Orchard Ridge*], your home has experienced exceptional appreciation. If you wish to explore the possibility of taking advantage of the market opportunities, we can supply you with a supported estimate of you home's present market value without any cost or obligation on your part.

I will be calling you in about a week to determine if you are interested in knowing what you could receive from a sale of your home.

Yours truly,

_____

**NOTE:** *By indicating you will be calling, you force the reader to consider his or her response. It is an extremely effective technique.*

*This flyer can be used for cold canvassing, but would be especially strong if mailed to persons having financial difficulties because of liens, foreclosures, divorce, death in the family, criminal action or automobile repossessions.*

*Consider enclosing the Free Market Analysis Certificate on page 19, with this flier.*

# Only Seven Days to Sell

---

### Only Seven Days to Sell

That's right, it took just [*seven*] days for [*Clyde Realty*] to sell the home of the [*Clarence Jones family*] at [*2738 West Wilson*]. [*We hope you will welcome your new neighbors Henry and Jean Watson. They have two children, Lisa, 9, and Henry, Jr., who is 6.*]*

If you want to know what your home would bring at a sale in today's market, call me for a computer-generated competitive market analysis. We supply this service without cost of obligation in the hope that when you consider selling you'll think of [*Clyde Realty*].

[*Henry Perkins*]
[*Sales Associate*]
[*Clyde Realty*]                                    [*555-8200*]

---

*\*This mailing should be restricted to the area of the sale.*

# We're Sold Out

**We're Sold Out**

We don't have a home to sell in [*name of subdivision*]. It is a case of demand just exceeding the supply.

If you are at all contemplating selling your home, you should consider acting now to take advantage of the favorable market.

What is your home worth in today's market? Call me today for a computer-generated competitive market analysis without any cost or obligation whatsoever, a service of [*Clyde Realty*].

[*Karen Schmidt*]
[*Sales Associate*]
[*Clyde Realty*]                                    [*555-8200*]

# I Apologize

### I Apologize

If you want to buy a home in [*Claridge Estates*], I don't really have much to show you. There has been a terrific demand, and the few owners who have taken advantage of the market quickly sold their homes. However, if you really want to buy, call me and I will put your name on my list of buyers.

Now, if you are interested in selling, that's a different story. Call me and I will prepare a computer printout of recent comparable sales for you, indicating the price range we can anticipate from a sale in the current market.

This service is at no cost or obligation to you. Because the market is affected by economic change, don't take a chance with your investment. Call today.

[*Henry Hopkins*]
[*Sales Associate*]
[*Clyde Realty*]                                    [*555-8200*]

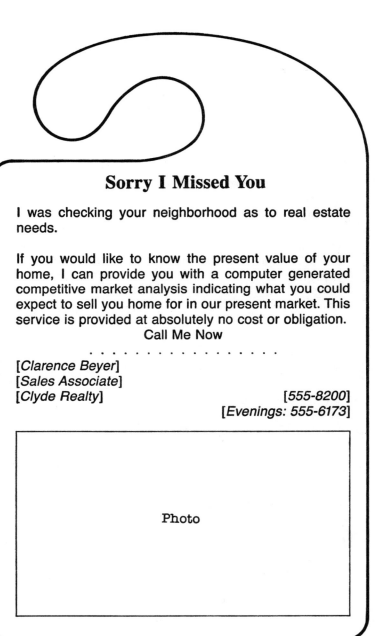

### Sorry I Missed You

I was checking your neighborhood as to real estate needs.

If you would like to know the present value of your home, I can provide you with a computer generated competitive market analysis indicating what you could expect to sell you home for in our present market. This service is provided at absolutely no cost or obligation.
### Call Me Now

. . . . . . . . . . . . . . . . .

*[Clarence Beyer]*
*[Sales Associate]*
*[Clyde Realty]*                           *[555-8200]*
                              *[Evenings: 555-6173]*

Photo

**NOTE:** *This is a "door hanger" to be used as a farming tool.
Consider perforating the door hanger so the business card
can be detached.*

# Graduation of Son or Daughter

[*Date*]

_____

_____

_____

Dear _____ :

Our congratulations! I bet you feel relieved your [*son*] [*daughter*] has graduated from [*high school*] [*college*]. Now, you will probably be able to think about your own needs.

Perhaps you want a smaller home, or the low-maintenance life in an apartment, condominium or mobile home. Perhaps you want to retire and head for a warmer climate. Whatever your housing needs are, I can help you.

Before you make any decisions, you should know exactly where you stand. I will be happy to furnish you with a [*computer-generated*] competitive market analysis that will indicate the present value of your home. In this way, you will know what to expect should you decide to sell. Call me today for this free analysis, offered without obligation.

Yours truly,

_____

**NOTE:** *The Free Market Analysis Certificate (page 19) could be enclosed with this letter.*

# Birth of Son or Daughter
## Condominium or Mobile Home Owner

[*Date*]

_____

_____

_____

Dear _____ :

Congratulations on the birth of your [*son, John*] [*daughter, Mary Jane*]. It won't be long before [*he*] [*she*] will be running around in seemingly perpetual motion. You will probably be considering purchasing a home with your own backyard for [*John*] [*Mary Jane*].

I can help you, not only in finding the perfect home, but also in selling your [*condominium*] [*mobile home*]. Our office provides a computer-generated competitive market analysis indicating what you could expect to receive on a sale of your [*condominium*] [*mobile home*] in today's market. We provide this service without any cost or obligation on your part. We can also analyze your finances and explain current lender requirements and possible loan limits.

I will be calling you in the next few days to discuss your housing needs.

Yours truly,

_____

**NOTE:** *From the addresses in birth announcements, you can ascertain if the parents live in condominiums or mobile homes. These parents are likely prospects for both a listing and a sale.*

# Marriage of Son or Daughter

[*Date*]

_____

_____

_____

Dear _____ :

Congratulations! Now that your [*son*] [*daughter*] is married, you probably have feelings of happiness mixed with feelings of relief and even sadness. It is, however, a time when you can begin thinking more about your own needs.

Perhaps you want a smaller home, a low-maintenance home or a different life-style. You may even be considering retirement. Whatever your housing needs are, I can help you.

Before you make any decision, you should know your complete financial picture. I'll be happy to prepare a computer-generated competitive market analysis, which will indicate the present value of your home. In this way, you will know what to expect should you decide to sell.

Call me today for this free analysis, offered without obligation on your part.

Sincerely,

_____

# Retirement

[*Date*]

_____

_____

_____

Dear _____ :

Congratulations on your retirement. I wish you many happy years to enjoy the fruits of your labor.

A great may retirees move to areas such as Florida for the mild climate, relaxed life-style and common interests of retirement communities, as well as the lower housing costs. Chances are you could sell your home, buy a nice home or condominium in Florida and have cash left over to invest to supplement your retirement income.

Before you make any decision, you should first know exactly where you stand. I will be happy to prepare a computer-generated competitive market analysis, which will indicate the value of your home in the present market. In this way, you will know what to expect should you decide to sell. Call me today for this free analysis, offered without obligation.

Yours truly,


_____


**NOTE:** *Employee newsletters are an excellent source of retiree information. Some personnel offices will also provide information.*

# Free Market Analysis Certificate

---

### Free Market Analysis

This certificate is good for one free computer-generated competitive market analysis indicating the likely sale price you could expect to receive for your home in today's marketplace.

This analysis is provided without any charge or obligation on your part to list or sell your home.

[*Bob Jones*]
[*Clyde Realty*]                                    [*555-8200*]

---

**NOTE:** *This certificate can be mailed to For Sale By Owner families as well as for general solicitations. It can also be used as an enclosure with other mailings.*

# A Neighbor Listed with Us

### Want to Know What
### Your Neighbors Did?

Your neighbors at [*111 Midvale Lane*] have just placed their home for sale through [*Clyde Realty*].

They will be able to take advantage of [*the exceptional demand our office has been experiencing in your area*] [*the current seller's market*] [*the rapid appreciation in value of the past few years*].

If you want to know what a sale of your home can mean for you in dollars and common sense, call me today.

[*Roberta Smith*]
[*Clyde Realty*]                                    [*555-8200*]

**NOTE:** *Besides soliciting listings, this flier lets neighbors know of the availability of the property and could also serve to locate buyers.*

# What's Happening in the Neighborhood

## We Are Zeroing in on Your Home

The following properties have been recently sold [around your home] [by Clyde Realty].

| | |
|---|---|
| [3BR Stardust Lane] | [$189,500] |
| [2BR Stardust Circle] | [$167,500] |
| [3BR Lynn Court] | [$214,500] |
| [4BR Lynn Court] | [$274,500] |

Would you like to see a "Sold" sign in front of your property as well?

Call [Tom Jones]
[Clyde Realty]  [555-8200]

for a free competitive market analysis indicating what you can expect to receive for a sale.

**NOTE:** *Consider enclosing the Free Market Analysis Certificate on page 19 with this flier.*

*Exact addresses of particular homes should not be given without permission of both buyer and seller.*

# There Goes the Neighborhood

---

### There Goes the Neighborhood

It must seem that way to you, since [*Clyde Realty*] has sold [*19*] homes in [*Truesdale Estates*] in the last [*6*] months.

There are good reasons for our phenomenal success in [*Truesdale Estates*], and I would like the opportunity to discuss them with you.

I would also like to prepare a competitive market analysis, which will indicate the likely sale price of your home in today's marketplace should you decide to sell. We perform this service without any cost of obligation on your part.

I will call you in a few days to see if I can be of any assistance to you in your real estate needs.

[*Tom Watkins*]
[*Associate Broker*]
[*Clyde Realty*]                              [*555-8200*]
                        Evenings: [*555-6138*]

---

# We Move Houses

## We Move Houses
## (No Size Limit)

We can find a new owner for your home and, if you wish, have you in a new home in record time.

Want to know how we do it and what you could expect to realize from a sale? Call me today for a free consultation.

Incidentally, we provide a computer-generated competitive market analysis indicating what you will likely receive from the sale of your home in today's marketplace. This service is provided free, without any obligation on your part.

[*Tom Brown*]
[*Sales Associate*]
[*Clyde Realty*]                    [*555-8200*]
                    Evenings: [*555-6138*]

# Help Us Find a Home for a Neighbor #1

---

### Can You Help a Neighbor?

We need a 3-bedroom home in your neighborhood for a [*young family*]. The [*husband is an engineer and the wife is a school teacher. They have a son 11 years old and a daughter who is seven. They would like to relocate prior to school in September and desire a home within walking distance of Midvale School*].

If you know of any friends or neighbors who might consider selling their home to this young family, we would appreciate hearing from you.

Sincerely,

[*Bob Jones*]
[*Clyde Realty*]

---

**NOTE:** *The heading should get this missive read. The family should be a real family with whom you are working, and they should be pictured in a very positive manner. People will go out of their way to help specific people, but not people in general. This is not only an effective listing canvassing tool, but the effort expended for the family you are working for will serve to make them feel indebted to you, reducing the chances of them contacting another agent.*

# Help Us Find a Home for a Neighbor #2

[Date]

_____

_____

_____

Dear _____ :

We are desperately in need of a [three-bedroom, two-bath] home [close to] [within walking distance of] [the First Midvale Congregational Church]. The home is needed for a [young family who have a son 9 years old and a daughter 7 years old. They are transferring to the area and would like to become members of your church].

Any assistance you can provide in helping us find a home for this fine family would be greatly appreciated.

Yours truly,

_____

_____

**NOTE:** *You want to picture the family in a very positive fashion. People like to help nice people, especially when they have common interests. This type of solicitation is extremely effective when your mailing is to the membership of the particular church. Because of the effectiveness of this directed solicitation you should consider asking prospective buyers if they would prefer to locate close to any particular church. By contacting the church, you should be able to obtain a membership list.*

# Help Us Find a Home for a Neighbor #3

[*Date*]

_____

_____

_____

Dear _____ :

[*Dirty old man with his child bride*] is desirous of obtaining a [*two- to three-bedroom home in the Clayton Hills area*]. He indicates he will pay up to [*$200,000, but there is probably some upward room as the old codger is loaded*]. If you are interested in unloading your house on him, call me today at [*476-8200*].

Passionately yours,


_____


**NOTE:** *This unusual type of solicitation was used successfully by Roy Brooks, an English broker, and it generated phenomenal response.*

*Before you prepare or use a letter such as this, obtain permission from the "dirty old man!"*

# Help Us Find a Home for a Neighbor #4

---

### Pretty Young Girl

who wants desperately to get married and start a family, has finally found a suitable mate.

Her problem is she has no place to keep him. If you would be willing to sell a [*3BR Westside home with a garage for $160,000 or less*], please call me immediately. The alternative is spinsterhood.

[*Tom Flynn, Sales Associate*]
[*Clyde Realty*]
[*555-8200*]

---

**NOTE:** *A light solicitation flier such as this for a particular buyer can be extremely effective. It is likely to be read and talked about.*

*And, as with the previous letter, make sure you get permission from the "pretty young girl" before you use this tactic.*

# Lady Saxophone Player

---

### Lady Saxophone Player
### With CASH

Needs a [*3BR, or 2BR and den*] home in [*West Encino*]. She will pay up to [*$140,000, but needs September 1 occupancy*].

If you or anyone you know would be interested in selling to her, please call me at once.

[*Tom Flynn*]
[*Sales Associate*]
[*Clyde Realty*]                                         [*555-8200*]

---

*NOTE:* *By taking a hobby or interest of a buyer, you can create a heading that will almost guarantee that the flier or letter will be read. Here are some examples: "Lady Sky Diver," "Middle-Aged Spelunker" or "She Plays with Dolls and Wants a Place to Keep Them."*

# Listing Solicitation—Out-of-Town Owner

[*Date*]

_____

_____

_____

Dear _____ :

As you undoubtedly know, owning property that is far away from you can be a real hassle.

Right now, we are experiencing an exceptional market. I believe we can sell your [*three-bedroom home*] in [*Midvale Heights*] at an attractive price.

I will be calling you in the next few days to ascertain your interests in selling the property.

Yours truly,


_____


**NOTE:** *The knowledge of an imminent call makes an owner consider the option of selling. This letter has greater effect if the property has vacancies, needs repair or has had recent evictions.*

# Listing Solicitation—Apartments

## Tenant Problems?

Have you considered the advantage of having your apartment equity in government bonds, tax-free municipals, or . . . ?

- No rents to try to collect
- No vacancies to worry about
- No repairs to make
- No tenant complaints
- No building inspector problems
- No evictions

I will be calling you in a few days to check your interest in selling. (If you are happy as a landlord, we can even sell you another building.)

Incidentally, we perform a computer-generated competitive market analysis at no cost or obligation to you, which will indicate what you can expect to receive from the sale of your apartment building.

Yours truly,

_____

**NOTE:** *Besides general mailings to owners of apartments, consider checking public records for problem property for evictions, unpaid taxes, code violations and so on.*

# Builder Solicitation—Building Permit

[*Date*]

_____

_____

_____

Dear _____ :

I was happy to learn that you have taken out a construction permit for another new home at _____ . The area has been developing well and we have had excellent sales activity in the neighborhood.

I believe the most effective new-home marketing effort really starts before construction begins. A plan review by a marketing person will often reveal that some costly features are not essential, while others can increase the home's saleability and sale price far beyond their additional cost. I will be calling you in a few days to schedule a meeting so we can discuss ways to ensure a quick sale and to maximize your profits as well.

Yours truly,

_____

**NOTE:** *This letter offers benefits to the reader. Mention of an impending call forces the reader to consider the thought of reviewing the plan features.*

# Chapter

# 3

# Responses to Owner Inquiries

# Response to Value Inquiry #1

[Date]

_____

_____

_____

Dear _____ :

Regarding your inquiry as to the value of your [lot]
[home][building] at _____ , I believe the current
market would support a selling price in the range between
$_____ and $_____ .

This value estimate is based on [list positive and/or negative attributes of the property] and the recent sale of
_____ for $ _____ , [address] for $ _____ ,
and [address] for $ _____ .

Because of the current market conditions, I would recommend a list price of $_____ and I have enclosed an
agency agreement reflecting this price. Please sign and
return —— copies to our office so we can commence our
efforts to obtain a buyer for your _____ .

Yours truly,


_____

Enclosure

---

**NOTE:** _The positive features should show you appreciate the property. Don't be picky on the negative features but list them
when you are certain the owner realizes they are present._

_Whenever you want an enclosure to be mailed back to you,
include a self-addressed envelope, preferably with prepaid
postage._

# Response to Value Inquiry #2

[*Date*]

_____

_____
_____

Dear _____ :

In response to your inquiry as to the value of your
property at [*111 Midvale Lane*], I have performed a
competitive market analysis, which considers recent
sales of similar properties, similar properties currently
on the market and similar properties that were not sold
at their listed prices. Based on the enclosed competitive
market analysis, I recommend that your property be
placed on the market at [*$175,000*]. I have also included
agency agreements reflecting this price.

I believe it is a particularly advantageous time to place
your property on the market because of [*the increase in
sales activity*] [*the opportunity to lock in the recent
appreciation in value*] [*the current higher interest rates,
which make seller financing so attractive*] [*the recent
reduction in interest rates*] [*the present demand for
homes in the area*]. Please sign and return [*two*] copies
of the agency agreement and we will immediately get
to work on marketing your [*three-bedroom home*].

Yours truly,


_____

Enclosures

# Response to Value Inquiry #3

[*Date*]

_____

_____

_____

Dear _____ :

[*$46,000*] cash to you is our estimate of what you will have after paying off the mortgage and all sales costs for a sale of your home at _____ .

This estimate is based on the enclosed computer-generated competitive market analysis indicating that your home should sell for [*$149,000*]. The seller's proceeds estimate (enclosed) shows the estimated deductions from the gross to arrive at the net.

I have enclosed agency agreements reflecting the [*$149,000*] sale price. If [*$46,000*] cash interests you, please sign and return [*two*] copies to our office so we can immediatly get to work on selling your home [*and take advantage of this favorable market*].

Yours truly,

_____

Enclosures

# Response to Value Inquiry
# —Poor Market Conditions

[*Date*]

_____

_____

_____

Dear _____ :

At the present time the number of sellers far exceeds buyers
for [*type of property*]. Unless you must sell, I would recommend you keep the property off the market at this time.

If you must sell, you will have to give your property a
competitive edge. Similar property is currently listed
between $_____ and $_____ , but are not
selling well even at the lower prices. This it verified
by the enclosed competitive market analysis. Therefore,
I would recommend an even lower listing price of
$_____ . Such a price will attract attention and is
likely to result in a sale even under our present market
conditions.

I have enclosed a listing for your property reflecting the
above price. Please sign and return [*two*] copies if you
wish to sell your property at this time.

Yours truly,



_____

Enclosures

---

**NOTE:** *The strength of this letter is its obvious honesty. If you get
the listing it will be a salable listing, not one likely to cost
you money. This suggestion of delay is an effective negative
approach when you know the seller will be taking a loss.*

# Response to Value Inquiry—Repairs Needed

[*Date*]

_____

_____

_____

Dear _____ :

I have carefully examined your home at _____ . The resulting competitive market analysis is enclosed.

While I am confident I will be able to find a buyer at the price indicated in my analysis, I think you should give serious consideration to some property repairs. I believe approximately $ _____ in repairs could result in an increase in the selling price of $ _____ . I would recommend these repairs:

[*1. Paint exterior.*]
[*2. Repair porch and railing.*]
[*3. Paint living room and kitchen (light colors).*]
[*4. Install new lighting fixture in kitchen.*]
[*5. Replace floor tile in bath.*]
[*6. Hang vinyl wall covering in bath.*]
[*7. Professionally clean carpets.*]

I would be happy to obtain bids for all of the work and also to assist you in obtaining any desired financing.

I have enclosed an agency agreement for the property, based on selling the property without any repairs. Please sign and return 2 copies. If you decide to go ahead with the work, we can adjust the price to reflect the improvements made.

Yours truly,

_____

Enclosures

═══════════════════════════════════════════

**NOTE:** *The choice is not to sign a listing or not sign it, but to make repairs or sell the property "as is."*

# About Our Firm

[*Date*]

_____

_____

_____

Dear _____ :

In answer to your inquiry about [*Clyde Realty*], I would like to tell you about our firm:

[*We have been in business for 26 years*] [*I have been engaged in the real estate business since 1970*]. [*We are one of the largest firms in the area, with 56 salespeople in three offices*]. [*We are a small firm specializing in ____.*] [*As a member in good standing of the ____ Multiple Listing Service, we are able to make your home available to _____ offices and more than _____ salespeople.*] [*Our success record has been exemplary over the past few years and based on the present market, I would expect continued success.*]

[*I have enclosed a competitive market analysis prepared for your home, showing what you could expect to receive at a sale. Also enclosed is an agency agreement reflecting our recommended sale price. Please sign and return two copies to us if you would like our firm to arrange a sale of your property.*]

I will be calling you in the next few days to see if there are any further questions you may have.

Yours truly,


_____

Enclosures

# Listing and Management—Apartment

[*Date*]

_____

_____

_____

Dear _____ :

I have completed an in-depth analysis of your apartment building at _____ . The enclosed competitive market analysis is based on:

[ 1. Raising the rents of units 1,3 and 7 $40 per month. Raising the rents of units 4, 6, 8, and 10 $20 per month as rents for these units are currently below market level.
  2. Painting vacant units 5 and 9 as well as replacing carpeting.
  3. Painting the exterior and performing needed landscaping work, including planting flowers].

We would be happy to take charge of all required work. Enclosed is a property management agreement as well as a listing agreement. Please sign and return [*two*] copies of each so that we can immediately start preparing your property for a favorable sale.

Yours truly,


_____

Enclosures

---

**NOTE:** *In selling apartments, having management authority will allow you to make the property move saleable and increase your likelihood of success.*

42

# Referral of Inquiry

[*Date*]

_____
_____
_____

Dear _____ :

I appreciate your considering [*Clyde Realty*] for market-ing your property at _____ .

However, because of [*the distance from our office*] [*the fact that we specialize in residential property*], it would not be fair to you for us to market your property. You need an agent who [*is more familiar with the area*] [*specializes in marketing rental property*].

We have, therefore, contacted [*Lynn Jones*] at [*Jones Realty*] about your property. Because of their [*location*] [*experience in marketing rental property*], I believe they can better meet your needs. [*Lynn Jones*] will be contact-ing you in the next few days.

Again, thank you for considering [*Clyde Realty*]. If we can be of service to you in the future, please feel free to contact me.

Yours truly,

_____

**NOTE:** *This letter treats a value inquiry as an offer of a listing. It increases the likelihood of the referral firm being able to obtain an agency agreement.*

# Refusal of Open Listing

[*Date*]

_____

_____

_____

Dear _____ :

Thank you very much for offering our firm an open listing on your property at _____ . We must, however, decline your kind offer. Our acceptance of an open listing would not be fair to you.

Experience has shown that property that is not listed exclusively seldom sells. No one advertises it and the property will only be shown when an agent doesn't have an exclusive agency property to fit a buyer's needs. To take such a listing would be deceiving you and would give you a false hope for sales success.

I have therefore included an exclusive right-to-sell agency agreement making [*Clyde Realty*] responsible for selling your [*home*]. If you are serious about wishing to sell, please sign and return [*two*] copies of the agreement.

Yours truly,


_____

Enclosure

---

**NOTE:** *You may also wish to include a competitive market analysis. To many, the term* agency agreement *brings forth an image of a helpful partnership, while* listing *has a more negative connotation.*

# Chapter

# 4

# Solicitations for For-Sale-by-Owner Listings

# The Owner's Quiz

### Can You Pass the Owner's Quiz?

Do you have a buyer?

Have you qualified him or her as to
financial ability?

Is your buyer contractually obligated to
the purchase?

Has your buyer been able to arrange the
necessary financing?

If all the answers are yes, then congratulations on your
sale. If you answered no to any of these questions, call
[555-8200] immediately. I will show you how [Clyde Re-
alty] can sell your home without any cost to you.

[Henry Fisk]
[Clyde Realty]

**NOTE:** You may wish to use one of the approaches from Power Real
Estate Listing [Real Estate Education Company, 1988] to
show the client how the buyer not the seller, really pays the
commission.

✓

# Full-Price Buyer

[*Date*]

_____

_____

_____

Dear _____ :

If I had a full-price buyer for your home, would you be willing to pay our fee?

If the answer is yes, call me immediately.

Yours truly,


_____

**NOTE:** *This short note will result in many responses. It provides a chance to be invited to view the premises and talk to the owner. Remember, you have not said you have a buyer; you only asked if the owner would pay a fee if you had one.*

*Don't address the letters to occupant. Reverse directories will help you determine the owner's name from an ad that uses a phone number or address.*

# Agents Sell

**Why Are Most For Sale By Owner Signs Replaced by Agent Signs?
Because Agents Sell!**

**Utilizing an agent means:**

- You are protected against unscrupulous buyers hoping to pay less than market value for your home.

- No unescorted, unqualified persons will enter your home.

- Contracts are likely to end in a sale—not in a courtroom.

- You are able to meet buyer financing needs.

- You are no longer a prisoner in your own home waiting for the bell to ring.

- You are more likely to sell your home.

- The sale will result in a higher net to you.

Think about it. I will be calling you in the next few days to answer any questions you might have and to prove everything I have said.

[*Tom Jones*]
[*Clyde Realty*]                    [*555-8200*]

# No Agent

---

### No Agent = No Commission

That seems like a good reason to try to sell without an agent—except that "no agent" usually means "no sale." That explains why most For Sale By Owner signs are replaced by agent signs.

I will be calling you in the next few days to show you not only the dangers of owner sales, but the positive benefits we can offer. If I can show you how I can put more money in your pockets, will you want to talk with me?

[*Joe Schmidt*]
[*Clyde Realty*]                                    [*555-8200*]

---

**NOTE:** *This is a short and effective letter. It grabs the reader's attention and states a common owner belief. Asking if the reader will talk to you to find out how to make more money from the sale of a home makes it hard to say no. When you call, you might say, "[Mr. Smith], I wrote you the other day and told you I would call. My letter asked if I could show you how I could put more money in you pockets – would you want to talk with me? I would like to show [both you and Mrs. Smith] how I will accomplish this. Will [both you and Mrs. Smith] be home [tonight at 7:00 P.M.], or would [8:00 P.M.] be more convenient?"*

*The choice given above is to time, not if they will talk with you. When you meet them, you would use material from Power Real Estate Listing [Longman], to show the seller the financial benefits of listing with your office.*

# Free Help

[*Date*]

_____

_____

_____

Dear _____ :

Could you use some free help?

Our office supplies [*purchase offer forms*] [*For Sale By Owner suggestions*] to owners who wish to sell their homes without the use of an agent. We do so without cost or obligation. We also provide a free estimate of value based on current documented sales.

No, we are not a charity—we do this in the hope that should you later decide to utilize an agent's services, you will remember our assistance.

I will be calling you within the next few days to set up an appointment so I can drop off the _____ with you and answer any questions you might have.

Yours truly,


_____

# Selling Without an Agent

### Selling Without an Agent?
### It Can Be Done, but Be Careful

I have enclosed a group of helpful hints and warnings that we have compiled to help owners who don't wish to use an agent. Study them carefully. Not only can they mean the difference between a sale and no sale, they can also protect you against a lawsuit or losing your home to an unscrupulous buyer.

If you want an explanation of any of this material or would like to know how you benefit financially and emotionally from being represented by an agent, please contact me.

I will check with you to see how you are doing and to offer whatever advice I can.

Yours truly,


[*Timothy Callahan*]
[*Sales Associate*]
[*Clyde Realty*]

Enclosure

**NOTE:** *Enclose "How To Sell Your Home Without an Agent," pages 56–58 with this letter.*

# The Story of Hazel

### Owner Sells Home
### Without Agent
### No Agent Fee Paid

Hazel Jones has just sold her three-bedroom, two-bath home and didn't have to pay a commission. It only took her 11 months and 42 open houses to do it. Hazel figures that after all advertising expenses she saved 79¢ an hour for her time.

Unfortunately, the buyer didn't pay cash. Hazel did receive some nice Confederate war bonds, due in 2020. Hazel is living proof the average seller doesn't need an agent.

I will call you in a few days to see if you want to be like Hazel.

[*Timothy Callahan*]
[*Sales Associate*]
[*Clyde Realty*]                              [*555-8200*]

**NOTE:** *This letter is, of course, a spoof to point out just a few of the For-Sale-By-Owner problems.*

# The Story of Homer

### Homer Fink Saves Thousands

Homer Fink is selling his home without an agent so he can save the agent's fee for himself. Homer is a pretty smart guy.

Of course, Homer stays home every evening and weekends waiting for the phone to ring, or the doorbell to buzz. Homer doesn't mind, as it keeps him from being out spending money and it gives his life a purpose, that of selling his home.

Homer can't understand why most of his hot prospects fail to return and talk of deals never ends up on paper. Nevertheless, Homer has faith that Mr. and Mrs. Right will come along. Anyway, he can always sell to the gentleman in the blue suede shoes who offered to trade him stock in an emerald mine.

If you want to be like Homer we wish you luck, but if you really want to sell, give some consideration to what I have to say when I call you in a few days.

[*Henry Wilson*]
[*Associate Broker*]
[*Clyde Realty*]                                    [*555-8200*]

# The Sign in Front of Your Home

---

### SOLD

Is this the sign in front of your home? Or is it simply,

### For Sale
### By Owner

The likelihood of turning the second sign into the first sign is very slim, which explains why most For Sale By Owner signs are replaced by broker's signs.

Did you realize that:

1. most calls on For Sale By Owner signs are from people who can't afford the home they are calling on?

2. most calls from newspaper ads are from people who would not be satisfied with a home priced in the range they inquired about?

Without an inventory to move inquiries up or down, most of an owner's effort ends up wasted.

I will call you in the next few days, not to try to saddle you with agent selling fees, but to show you how I can help you have more money in your pocket after a sale.

Isn't what you actually net more important than anything else?

[Tom Haskins]
[Sales Associate]
[Clyde Realty]                                [555-8200]

---

### How To Sell Your Home Without an Agent

1. Change ads regularly. Ads lose effect if repeated without change. Three days is plenty for one ad. Rewrite ads to appeal to different categories of likely buyers. Use plenty of adjectives. Spend time writing, as your ad competes with many ads for similar property.

2. Obtain purchase contract forms (Call our office if you do not have any.) Complete the purchase contract except for date, price, terms and signatures. Make certain you fully understand every provision. If a prospective buyer wants to use his or her own contract, be alert. Take it to an attorney. What might appear to be a standard form could be one-sided and not say what it appears to say. With desktop publishing, many wheeler-dealers are using their own forms where the small print taketh away what the large print giveth.

3. Check financing on at least a weekly basis (mortgage company) so you will be able to help a buyer understand his or her down payments and monthly costs for various types of mortgages tailored to the buyer's needs. You will need to buy an amortization table from your local bookstore. Be prepared to explain loan types to prospective buyers. There are many excellent texts available to help you.

4. If a prospective buyer uses the words *subordinate* or *subordination* in the offer, turn and run. If you sign, no matter how good it looks, you are likely giving away your home to a charlatan. Also, be alert for any deals that seem too good to be true—they generally are. Be particularly alert with any buyer who is buying without any of his or her own cash. If the buyer ends up with more

cash than he or she started with, you can be certain you have been had. A number of fast-talking seminar promoters have instructed thousands in unethical and often illegal procedures. Offers of mortgages on other property, notes, colored stones, diamonds (especially uncut) or other claimed valuables should send you running to an attorney. If you don't have one, I would be happy to recommend several. When an agent is involved, the fast operators don't waste their time. They love For Sale By Owners.

5. Be certain you have considered and fully understand the effect of seller discount points, pay-off penalties on existing loans, assumability of loans, ownership of the impound account and advantages of having fire insurance policies assumed rather than a short-rate cancellation. Understand the dangers of "subject-to" financing as opposed to loan assumptions.

6. Make certain you are prepared with all seller disclosures mandated by state law.

7. Make certain you fully understand the requirements of state and federal fair housing legislation.

8. Make certain you know who a prospective buyer is before he or she crosses your threshold. There have been too many horror cases of trusting home owners opening their homes to persons with intentions other than to buy, and treating them as if they were honored guests.

9. Beware of contingent offers. The property could be tied up for months or even years. The buyer could be a dealer who wants to hold the property as if it were an option that would only be exercised if another buyer is located.

*continued on following page*

---

*continued from preceding page*

10. How did you arrive at your price? Unless you have a written competitive market analysis considering all recent sales of comparable property, your price could be merely a hunch. Too high a price will almost certainly guarantee that your property will not be sold and you will be simply wasting time and effort, and too low a price will mean you are giving away dollars that are rightfully yours. You want a realistic price that gives you an advantage over your competition, creating interest in your property. You should then hold to your price with only minor concessions.

11. Understand fully the tax consequences of the sale. Have you considered the advantages of a tax-free exchange where you choose the property you receive? Have you considered the tax benefit of providing some seller financing on an installment sale?

If you are determined to sell your home yourself, we wish you good luck. If you want to know the advantages I can offer, call me.

[*Clyde Realty*]

---

**NOTE:** *This form can be used as a handout and an enclosure with other For-Sale-by-Owner letters.*

# Owners Who Have Homes for Rent

---

### Do You Really Want To Rent?

Consider these points:

- Rental income seldom makes economic sense when compared to the likely sale price.

- When you rent your home, you are placing a tenant in charge of a valuable asset. Consider the dangers of a tenant who is not caring.

Let us show you how we can sell your home now and what you could expect to receive from a sale. We furnish a computer-generated market analysis without any cost or obligation on your part. Call me today at [*555-8200*].

[*Jane Thomas*]
[*Clyde Realty*]

---

**NOTE:** *Another effective final sentence might be: "I will be contacting you in the next few days to discuss the advantages that a sale offers you over renting."*

√

# For Sale By Owner—
## Unsuccessful Listing Attempt #1

[*Date*]

_____

_____

_____

Dear _____ :

Thank you so very much for the opportunity to visit your beautiful home in [*Westwood*]. As I indicated, I believe [*Clyde Realty*] can be of service to you in helping to find the perfect family that will appreciate all your home has to offer.

I will be contacting you again in a few weeks to check on your sale progress and to see if I can help you in your efforts.

Yours truly,


_____

# Unsuccessful Listing Attempt #2

[*Date*]

_____

_____

_____

Dear _____ :

I would like to thank you for the opportunity to view your lovely home [*this past Thursday*]. I am certain that, if given the opportunity, we would be able to find a buyer for your home who will be willing to pay a reasonable value.

If there are any questions you may have about selling your home, please do not hesitate to contact me. I will contact you again in about a week to see how your efforts are going.

Yours truly,

_____

**NOTE:** *A good time for a personal follow-up contact is late on a Sunday afternoon after an unsuccessful open house.*

# Chapter

# 5

# Servicing the Listing

✓

# Thank You for Listing #1

[Date]

_____

_____

_____

Dear _____ :

As the broker with [Clyde Realty], I would like to let you know that I appreciate the confidence you have shown by making [Clyde Realty] your exclusive agent for the sale of your home.

I want you to know we will use our best efforts to locate a buyer at the highest price and best terms possible for you. Besides our own sales force, your home will be made available to other agents through our multiple listing service, so in effect you will have [107] offices and [852] salespersons working on your behalf.

[Janet Jones] will keep in contact with you as to advertising, showings and suggestions for improving the salability of your home. If you have any questions at all, please contact [him] [her] or me.

I am looking forward to meeting your needs with a completed sale.

Yours truly,

_____

# Thank You for Listing #2

[*Date*]

_____

_____

_____

Dear _____ :

I appreciate the trust you have shown in [*Clyde Realty*] by appointing us your agent for the sale of your [*home*].

I want you to know you can expect diligent and professional efforts on our part to effectuate a favorable sale of your [*home*]. We have already [*prepared initial advertising*] [*placed initial advertising*] and provided information on your home [*to our multiple listing service*]. We will keep in touch with you as to our efforts and the results. [*Mr. Lynn Smith*] of our office will be working with you throughout the sales process and even after the sale to make certain there is a satisfactory closing. If you have any questions concerning your property or our efforts, please contact [*Mr. Smith*].

I look forward to being able to present you with a buyer.

Yours truly,

_____

# Thank You for Listing—Out-of-Town Owner

[*Date*]

_____

_____

_____

Dear _____ :

I would like to thank you for showing your confidence in
[*Clyde Realty*] by appointing us your exclusive agent for
the sale of your property. We have already entered your
[*home*] on the multiple listing service computer. Your
[*home*] is now available to [*712*] agents in [*57*] offices.

Because you live a great distance from our office, could
you please provide us with the following information?

1. The name of a local person to contact in the event of
   an emergency
2. The name of your insurance agent (property insurance) and policy number

You should contact your insurance agent to make certain
you have adequate coverage.

I look forward to being able to tell you that your [*home*]
has been sold.

Sincerely,

_____

# Neighborhood Information Request

[*Date*]

_____
_____
_____

Dear _____ :

Having an in-depth knowledge of your neighborhood and neighbors can give us a competitive advantage over less informed sales agents who represent other properties.

We would therefore appreciate your completion of this form to the best of your ability.

1. Neighborhood features you feel a buyer would likely be most pleased with: _____
_____
_____

2. School districts are: _____
_____

3. School bus stops at: _____
_____

4. Names, ages and schools attended by neighboring children (include private schools):

_____ _____ _____
_____ _____ _____
_____ _____ _____
_____ _____ _____
_____ _____ _____

5. Youth activities in the area (Little League, junior hockey, soccer league, etc.): _____
_____
_____

6. Public recreational facilities in area (parks, pools, playgrounds, tennis courts, etc.): _____
_____
_____

7. Nearest public transportation route: _____
   _____

8. Nearest medical facility: _____
   _____

9. Nearest community center (for children, seniors,
   etc.): _____
   _____

10. Nearest churches (and denominations): _____
    _____
    _____

11. Nearest shopping area: _____
    _____

12. General information on closest neighbors: _____
    _____
    _____

13. People living in area that might interest a possible
    buyer (doctor, banker, attorney, professor or another
    professional): _____
    _____
    _____

14. Describe the type of person you feel would best
    appreciate your home and neighborhood: _____
    _____

Please send your completed form to my attention in the
enclosed postage-paid envelope.
Your help in providing this data is greatly appreciated.

Appreciatively yours,


_____


================================================

**NOTE:** *Not only does this letter gain you sales ammunition, it will
also show the owner you appreciate the neighborhood and
neighbors and are using your best efforts in their behalf.*

# Instruction Sheet Transmittal

[*Date*]

_____

_____

_____

Dear _____ :

In marketing your home, we are competing against
[*dozens*] [*hundreds*] of other owners who are all after a
much smaller pool of buyers. To compete successfully, we
want every advantage possible. The enclosed instruction
sheet will allow you to play an important role in obtaining
the best possible sale for your home.

Please let me know if you have any questions.

Yours truly,


_____

Enclosure

# Home Owner Instructions

### Home Owner Hints for a Successful Sale

I. Exterior

  A. Grass and shrubs: Keep trimmed. Consider a fast greening fertilizer such as ammonium sulfate (inexpensive) for a deep green lawn.

  B. Pets: If you have a dog, clean up any dog dirt on a daily basis. Secure pets when the house is being shown.

  C. Fences: Make any needed repairs. A neat, well-painted fence gives a positive impression.

  D. Flowers: Plant seasonal blooming flowers, especially near the front door and in any patio area. A profusion of color can have your home half-sold before the door is even opened.

  E. Bird feeders: Hummingbird feeders and bird houses create a pleasant mood, especially when they are close to any patio area.

  F. Paint:

    1. Front door should be refinished or painted if it shows excessive wear.

    2. Check exterior paint. Often, only the trim or, depending on sun exposure, only one or two sides of the house need painting. Keep in mind the fact that paint is cheap compared to the extra dollars a home with a clean fresh appearance will bring.

  G. Lawn furniture: Place lawn furniture in an attractive, leisurely manner. A badminton net or croquet set-up gives a positive image as well.

  H. Roof: If the roof needs to be repaired or replaced, it's best to have the work done. Otherwise, buyers

*continued on following page*

*continued from preceding page*

will want to deduct the cost even if your price already reflects the required work. Delaying repairs can actually cost you twice as much.

II. Interior

A. Housekeeping: You are competing against model homes, so your home must look as much like a model as possible. Floors, bath fixtures and appliances must be sparkling. Consider using a car wax on appliances. Make beds early in the day. Unmade beds and late sleepers create a very negative image.

B. Odors and aromas: Avoid using vinegar as well as heavy frying or cooking strong-smelling foods such as cabbage. The odors last and work against the image you are trying to create. On the other hand, some smells have a positive effect on people: Baked bread, apple pie, chocolate cookies and cinnamon rolls are examples of foods that can help sell your home. Consider keeping packaged cookie or bread dough in the refrigerator. Just before a scheduled showing, the smell of these baking foods can be a great help to us.

C. Paint: If you have leftover paint, you can accomplish a great deal by touching up paint where needed. If the paint is dark, repaint with light colors such as off-white, oyster, light beige or pale yellow. Light colors make rooms appear fresh as well as larger.

D. Plumbing: Repair any leaky faucets. Make certain you don't have a gurgling toilet.

E. Shades and blinds: Replace any torn shades or broken blinds.

F. Drapes: If drapes need cleaning, have it done. If they are old and worn, stained or dark consider replacing them with light colors. (Large department stores or catalog houses will generally solve the problem.)

G. Carpets: Dirty carpets should be either professionally steam cleaned (preferred), or you should rent a heavy-duty cleaner.

H. Lighting: If any room appears dark, increase the wattage of your light bulbs. Before a showing, open the blinds and drapes and turn on the lights, even during the day. You want the house as light as possible. Make certain your light fixtures and windows are clean.

I. Closets: If closets appear crowded, remove items not needed and put in boxes. They can be stacked neatly in a corner of the basement, attic or garage.

J. Too much furniture: Many homes appear crowded, with too many pieces of large furniture as well as bric-a-brac. Consider putting excess furniture in a storage locker.

K. Garage and basement: Spruce up your work area. Consider a garage sale to get rid of the excess items too good to throw away but of no use to you. Put excess items in boxes and stack them neatly in a corner. Consider using a commercial garage floor cleaner on excess oil and grease marks on the garage floor and driveway. You might consider a commercial steam cleaner (not carpet cleaner).

L. Temperature: On cold days, a natural fire in the fireplace will help us sell your home. Start the fire before the showing is scheduled. On hot days,

*continued on following page*

*continued from preceding page*

consider turning the air conditioner four to five degrees cooler than normal. The contrast will seem phenomenal, giving a very positive reaction. In moderate weather, open windows for fresh air.

III.  You

When your home is shown, it's best that you disappear for a while. Buyers feel restrained with an owner present. If buyers will not voice their concerns, then their questions cannot be answered and their problems cannot be solved.

If you must remain in the house, try to stay in one area. Excellent places to be are working in the garden, on the lawn or in the workshop. These activities create a positive image. While soft music is fine, do not have a TV on.

*Never, never* follow the agent around the house during the showing, volunteer any information or answer questions the buyers may have. You have engaged professional real estate salespersons. We will ask you questions if necessary.

*[Clyde Realty]*                                        [*555-8200*]

✓

# Seller's Net Proceeds Estimate Transmittal

[*Date*]

_____
_____
_____

Dear _____ :

Enclosed is a seller's net proceeds work sheet I have prepared for your property at _____ .

The net reflects [*your present mortgage being paid off and a sale at the list price of $*_____ ].

The figures provided are believed to be reliable, but are an estimate only and are not guaranteed.

If you have any questions, please contact me.

Yours truly,

_____

Enclosure

# Seller Net Proceeds Estimate Work Sheet

Credits:

| Sale price | $ ___ |
| Impound account balance | $ ___ |
| Prepaid insurance | $ ___ |
| _____ | $ ___ |
| Total credits | $ ___ |
| Total debits | $ ___ |
| Seller net* | $ ___ |

Debits:

| Loans being assumed | $ ___ |
| Loan prepayment penalties | $ ___ |
| Agent fees | $ ___ |
| Escrow/attorney | $ ___ |
| Abstract/title insurance | $ ___ |
| Transfer tax | $ ___ |
| Termite inspection | $ ___ |
| _____ | $ ___ |
| Miscellaneous | $ ___ |
| Total debits | $ ___ |

*NOTE: *Seller net cash and carryback financing where the seller is financing the buyer.*

# Ad Copy Transmittal

[*Date*]

_____

_____

_____

Dear _____ :

Enclosed is a copy of a classified advertisement, which appeared in the _____ on _____ .

I am certain you realize we receive many inquiries from our institutional advertising as well as from ads for specific property. What you may not be aware of is the fact that few buyers actually end up purchasing the home they originally inquired about. After qualifying a buyer as to needs and financial standing, it is common to find that the inquiry property does not fit the particular buyer. The buyer then is generally shown a number of other properties. In this way, every ad we place within a general price range serves as a sales tool for every home we have within that price range.

I want you to understand that we intend to promote the sale of your home to the best of our ability. All of our advertisements work to the advantage of your property, even those not specifically for it. We have proven that our advertising methods work in the past, and I feel confident they will be successful for your home.

Yours truly,

_____

Enclosure

# Progress Report

[*Date*]

_____

_____

_____

Dear _____ :

This note is to keep you informed of our efforts on your behalf.

During the month of _____ , we:

1. Advertised your home [*in 2 newspapers*] using [*3*] ads with insertions on [*11*] days. (This is in addition to our institutional advertising and ads for other property in the same price range.)

2. Have had more than [*50*] inquiries on your home and have had [*7*] showings by our own salespersons.

3. Have had [*5*] showings by salespersons from cooperating offices.

4. Have had [*one*] open house and registered [*17*] guests.

5. Your home has remained active in the Midvale Multiple Listing Service available to [*107*] offices and more than [*1,000*] salespersons.

[*While we have not yet received an offer on your home*], we are very optimistic as to the future and will continue our efforts on your behalf.

Yours truly,


_____

# Change of Agents

[*Date*]

_____

_____

_____

Dear _____ :

[*Mr. Keith Swift*] of our office will be taking over the
primary responsibility of the sale of your home from
[*Karen Jones*], who is no longer with our office. [*Mr.
Swift*] will be contacting you in the next few days to
discuss our past and future efforts on your behalf.

If you have any questions at all, please do not hesitate
to contact either me or [*Mr. Swift*].

Yours truly,

_____

# New Competitive Market Analysis

[*Date*]

_____

_____

_____

Dear _____ :

Because of the changing real estate marketplace, we have just completed the enclosed updated competitive market analysis of the value of your home.

From the sale's figures of comparable homes recently sold, as well as from the asking prices of similar homes that remain unsold, you will see that homes priced above the present market value are not selling. You will also see the necessity for a price adjustment to conform with market conditions. It is, after all, the marketplace that ultimately determines what a property will sell for.

I have enclosed a [*new listing*] [*listing addendum*] reflecting the current real estate market. Please sign and return [*two*] copies to our office.

Yours truly,

_____

Enclosure

**NOTE:** *It is better to blame the market rather than the home for the fact that a property has not sold. Never suggest lowering a price—the price is "adjusted" to reflect the market.*

*Generally, any request to adjust a listing price should be made in person rather than by letter.*

# Lender Appraisal below List Price

[*Date*]

_____

_____

_____

Dear _____ :

I have just received the enclosed appraisal by [*Midvale Savings and Loan*] on your home.

While I may not fully agree with this appraisal, it will nevertheless significantly affect prospective buyers, who will be reluctant to buy at a price above their lenders appraisal.

I therefore believe it is in your best interests to adjust the price to reflect this appraisal. I have enclosed an addendum reflecting the new price. Please sign and return [*two*] copies.

If you have any questions, do not hesitate to call me.

Yours truly,


_____

Enclosures

**NOTE:** *Never suggest lowering a price—the price is "adjusted" to reflect the lender's appraisal. Generally, any request to adjust a listing price should be made in person rather than by letter.*

√

# Price Adjustment Request—
# Property Listed above Appraisal

[*Date*]

_____
_____
_____

Dear _____ :

At the time we listed your home for sale at [*111 Midvale Drive*], our competitive market analysis indicated a market value of [*$125,500*]. Based on your decision as owner, the house was placed on the market at [*$150,500*].

Your home has now been on the market for [*90*] days, during which we have advertised the property, called prospective buyers to discuss it, [*held an open house*] and provided the listing information to a multiple listing service available to [*93*] offices and [*1,141*] agents. Despite our best efforts, we have seen little interest in your home. Those who have seen it have expressed the opinion that your home, while desirable, is overpriced compared to other available properties.

Therefore, it is our professional judgment that the price should be adjusted to [*$125,500*], the figure indicated by our competitive market analysis. If you truly want to sell your home, I am certain you will agree. I have enclosed a listing addendum that reflects this adjustment. Please sign and return [*two*] copies to my office.

Yours truly,

_____

Enclosure

✓

# Price Adjustment Request—
# Based on Competition

[*Date*]

_____
_____
_____

Dear _____ :

I would like to bring you up-to-date on several recent events. The property at [*5 Crescent Lane*], which is very similar to your [*home*], has just been placed on the market at ($_____). The property at [*532 Jupiter Avenue*], which was listed at ($_____) has just been sold for ($_____).

There appears to be a softening of the market, which greatly reduces the likelihood of selling your home at the list price of ($_____). If your home is to compete successfully in this market it is strongly suggested that the price be adjusted to ($_____). I have included a listing addendum reflecting this adjustment. Please sign and return [*two*] copies to this office.

Yours truly,

_____

Enclosure

**NOTE:** *The letter is not critical of the property, which would result in a negative reaction, it is the market that is at fault. A "price adjustment" is requested rather than a price reduction, which would mean the seller would have to give something up. Since this list price was only an estimate of the sale price, a change in the list price is not a reduction. Nothing the owner had is being taken away.*

# Price Adjustment—Request
# To Raise Price Based on Market Competition

[*Date*]

_____

_____

_____

Dear _____ :

Recent sales have indicated home prices are escalating.
We therefore prepared a new competitive market analysis
for your home at [*111 Midvale Trail*].

You'll see that it indicates our current asking price is too
low. While the low price would likely mean a very quick
sale, we feel we can get you a higher price within a
reasonable period of time.

I have included a listing addendum reflecting a price
adjustment to [*$250,000*]. Please sign and return [*2*]
copies to this office.

Yours truly,


_____

Enclosures

# Price Adjustment—Fixer-Upper

[*Date*]

_____

_____

_____

Dear _____ :

The current condition of your home at [*55 Lynn Court*] has made a sale difficult in our current market. As you know, [*the house needs decorating, the carpets need replacing and the home generally is showing the effects of its age*]. Unless you are willing to extensively rehabilitate the property, I would like your permission to advertise your home as a fixer-upper. This type of ad has strong appeal to many buyers who are not afraid of hard work.

To attract this type of buyer, a price adjustment would be necessary. I suggest a price of [*$96,000*], and I have enclosed a listing addendum that reflects this adjusted price. Please sign and return [*two*] copies to this office.

I am confident that taking this approach will mean a timely sale of your property. If you have any questions, please contact me.

Yours truly,


_____

Enclosure

---

**NOTE:** *Again, the preferred method of communicating a request for a price adjustment is by personal contact.*

√

# Request for Minor Repairs

[*Date*]

_____

_____

_____

Dear _____ :

Several prospective buyers who have visited your home
have commented about the [*broken porch railing*]. While
this is not a major problem, it nevertheless presents a
significant negative image to prospective buyers. We feel it
would be in your best interests to arrange for the necessary repair as soon as possible.

Yours truly,

_____

# Request for Minor Repairs
## —Nonresident Owner

[*Date*]

_____

_____

_____

Dear _____ :

Your [*home*] at _____ needs some mainte-
nance work and repairs including: _____
_____ .

Enclosed is an estimate of $_____ for the necessary
work. If you will forward your check for this amount, we
will see that the work is accomplished. While the work
suggested might appear minor in nature, having your
[*home*] in the best condition possible will contribute to
its salability as well as the sale price. When homes need
work, buyers tend to believe the owner is desperate, and
they are likely to reduce any offer they might otherwise
make.

We look forward to being able to place our "Sold" sign in
front of your [*home*].

Yours truly,


_____

Enclosure

# Request for Listing Extension

[*Date*]

_____

_____

_____

Dear _____ :

The activity has been increasing on your home, and I feel certain we will be successful in arranging a sale. We have been utilizing our best efforts on your behalf because we realize how important a sale is to you. During the last [ _____ ] months, we have placed numerous advertisements, held open houses and provided information on your home to over [ _____ ] offices and [ _____ ] salespeople.

We want to continue our efforts until we are successful. I have enclosed an extension to our agency agreement. Please sign and return [ _____ ] copies immediately so we can continue our efforts to consummate a sale without interruption.

Yours truly,


_____

Enclosure

---

**NOTE:** *Generally, a request for a listing extension should be made in person. It is much easier to say no to a letter than it is to a person.*

# Listing Extended—Thank-You

[ *Date* ]

_____

_____

_____

Dear _____ :

I would like to personally thank you for the confidence you have shown in [ *Clyde Realty* ] by extending our agency agreement on your [ *home* ] at _____ .

I want you to know we are using our efforts to the utmost in locating a buyer. We realize how much a sale means to you. I feel certain we shall succeed in our quest for a buyer.

Yours truly,

_____

**89**

✓

# Listing Expired—Thank You for Listing

[*Date*]

_____

_____

_____

Dear _____ :

I am very sorry you have decided not to renew our agency agreement. However, I want to thank you for having given [*Clyde Realty*] the opportunity to serve as your sales agent.

[*The market conditions were not favorable for a sale at the list price, although there is now an improvement in market conditions. I feel a listing extension would result in a sale. In the present market, I recommend you ask no more than $_____ for your home.*]

Should you change your mind and wish to utilize the services of [*Clyde Realty*] again, I have enclosed an agency agreement. By signing and returning [ _____ ] copies to our office, you will once again be certain we will utilize our best efforts to serve your interests. [*The new agency agreement reflects our recommendations.*]

Yours truly,

_____

Enclosure

# Purchase Offer Transmittal #1

[*Date*]

_____

_____

_____

Dear _____ :

It took a lot of effort, but we were successful in obtaining the enclosed offer on your [*house*]. I believe it to be a reasonable offer, as it provides you with [*93%*] of your asking price.

If you agree with me, please sign and return [ _____ ] copies in the enclosed envelope immediately. The buyers are not legally bound to this purchase until they receive a signed acceptance. Until that time, they have the right to cancel this offer.

Yours truly,

_____

**NOTE:** *Showing the offer as a percentage of the list price tends to minimize the difference.*

*A sense of urgency is created by correctly pointing out that a buyer can back out prior to acceptance. While sellers may refuse low offers, they don't like to allow the buyer to back out once an offer is made.*

# Purchase Offer Transmittal #2

[*Date*]

_____

_____

_____

Dear _____ :

I told you we would find a buyer, and I am now proud to present you with the enclosed offer. While it is not everything we desired, because of market conditions, I believe it is an exceptionally good sale.

Please sign and return [ _____ ] copies to me at once. As soon as I can notify the buyers of your acceptance, they will become legally bound to their purchase. Prior to this notification, they still have the right to revoke their offer.

Yours truly,

_____

Enclosure

# Purchase Offer Transmittal #3

[*Date*]

_____

_____

_____

Dear _____ :

I am proud to enclose a full-price purchase offer from
[*Janet Smith*]. [*The only deviation from your requirement
is that Ms. Smith has requested a 60-day escrow.*]

Prior to being notified of your acceptance, [*Ms. Smith*]
could conceivably revoke her offer; therefore, please sign
and return [ _____ ] copies at once.

Yours truly,

_____

Enclosure

# Low Purchase Offer—Transmittal

[*Date*]

_____
_____
_____

Dear _____ :

I have enclosed an offer we have received on your property
at _____ . The offer is not what we had hoped it
would be. You now have three options:

1. Acceptance, which would form a binding contract,
   and your home is sold.
2. Outright rejection, which would end the negotiation
   process.
3. Making a counteroffer. You should realize once a
   counteroffer is made, you can no longer accept the
   earlier offer, as that offer is considered to be dead.
   The buyers then have the option of accepting or
   rejecting your counteroffer.

If you feel you can't risk losing this buyer, I would recommend acceptance rather than making a counteroffer. If
you can take the risk, I would recommend a counteroffer
at $_____ , based on current market conditions,
although the amount of the counteroffer is your decision.

Besides the offer, which can be accepted by your signature,
I have also prepared a counteroffer reflecting my recommendations. Please sign and return _____ copies of
whichever set of forms you decide to go with.

Yours truly,

_____

Enclosures

# Poor Offer—Transmittal

[Date]

_____

_____

_____

Dear _____ :

As your agent, I am required to submit every offer received. The enclosed offer to purchase is therefore transmitted to you.

I recommend the offer be rejected as being unreasonable [with a counteroffer for $ _____ , which is enclosed for your signature] [without any counteroffer].

While you have the right to accept the offer and form a binding contract, I hope you will follow my advice, as I do not think an acceptance would be in your best interest.

Yours truly,

_____

[Enclosure]

**NOTE:** _If there were specific problems with the offer such as dangerous clauses like subordination agreements, or the offer involved unsecured notes or trades of property having questionable value, the problems should be specifically pointed out._

# Seller Net Proceeds Estimate—
## After Offer

[*Date*]

_____

_____

_____

Dear _____ :

Enclosed is a seller net proceeds work sheet that I have
prepared for your property, based on the $ _____
offer of _____ .

The figures provided are believed to be reliable, but are not
guaranteed.

If you have any questions, please contact me.

Yours truly,


_____

Enclosure

---

**NOTE:** *See page 76 for enclosure.*

# Offer Rejected

[*Date*]

_____

_____

_____

Dear _____ :

I'm very sorry the offer we received on your [*home*] failed to meet your expectations. As you know, we are your agents and as agents we have a duty to present every offer received.

I want you to know we will continue with our best efforts to sell your [*home*], and we remain hopeful of an early success.

Yours truly,

_____

# Information Letter—Status of Sale

[*Date*]

_____

_____

_____

Dear _____ :

[*The financing has been approved*] for [*Janet Jones*]
[*The Joneses*], the purchaser[*s*] of your [*home*].

I will be contacting you within a few days to give you
closing information.

Yours truly,


_____

# Removal of Contingency

[*Date*]

_____
_____
_____

Dear _____ :

This is to notify you that [*The Joneses*] have signed the enclosed contingency release. Their purchase agreement now stands without the contingency of [*obtaining an 11 percent loan for 80 percent of the purchase price*].

Yours truly,

_____

Enclosure

# Failure of Buyer Contingency

[*Date*]

_____

_____

_____

Dear _____ :

In accordance with our phone conversation, [*Mr. and Mrs. Smith*] have been unable to [*obtain financing*] in accordance with the contingency set forth in their purchase offer.

Please sign the enclosed release forms so that I can return their deposit in accordance with our agreement.

We have resumed our sales efforts and are confident of success in selling your home.

Yours truly,


_____

Enclosure

---

**NOTE:** *When it appears a contingency will not be met, let the owner know immediately so that failure will not come as a shock. Be certain the seller agrees to the return of deposit before it is returned. A court could otherwise later decide the failure to meet the contingency was the fault of the buyer. If this is the case, you could be held liable for the returned deposit.*

# Closing Documents Transmittal— to Buyer or Seller

[*Date*]

_____

_____

_____

Dear _____ :

Enclosed are the following documents for [*your signature*] [*both of your signatures*]:

_____

_____

_____

_____

Please sign where indicated.

Important: [ _____

_____ ] and [ _____ ] must be [*signed in the presence of a notary public*].

Please return the documents as indicated by _____ .

Yours truly,

_____

Enclosures

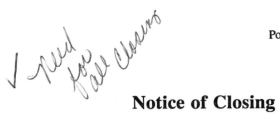

# Notice of Closing

[*Date*]

_____

_____

_____

Dear _____ :

The closing for the sale of your home at _____ will take place at [*our office at 9 A.M.*] on [*August 6*]. It is necessary that both owners be present. The following checklist may be of help to you:

☐ Notify the post office of your change of address.
☐ Notify magazines, credit card companies, friends, etc., of your address change.
☐ Cancel subscriptions to newspapers, or let them know of your change of address.
☐ Cancel service contracts (such as pest control, gardener or water softener company).
☐ Cancel or transfer any insurance coverage.
☐ Disconnect or transfer utilities:
    ☐ Water
    ☐ Gas
    ☐ Electricity
    ☐ Phone
    ☐ Cable TV
    ☐ Trash
☐ Leave all warranties and manuals for appliances.
☐ Leave extra keys.
☐ Leave garage door openers.

If you have any questions concerning the closing, please contact me.

Yours truly,

_____

# Settlement Statement Transmittal

[*Date*]

_____

_____

_____

Dear _____ :

Enclosed is your check for $ _____ as well as your settlement statement for the sale of your property at [ *77 Lynn Court* ].

We hope to be able to serve you for any future real estate needs.

Yours truly,


_____

Enclosures

# Request for Return of Personal Property

[*Date*]

_____

_____

_____

Dear _____ :

The [*Smiths*] are now in their new home and are delighted with it. You certainly took excellent care of this fine home.

We do have a minor problem, in that the [*dining room ceiling fan*] was not in the house when the [*Smiths*] took possession. Your movers might have inadvertently packed it. As you realize, [*the purchase contract called for the ceiling fan to stay*] [*the listing made a positive point of the ceiling fan remaining*] [*the ceiling fan is regarded as a fixture, which must be left with the house unless agreed otherwise*].

Please pack and return the [*ceiling fan*] to the [*Smiths*] as soon as practical. Thanking you in advance for your prompt attention to this matter.

Yours truly,

_____

**NOTE:** *This is a diplomatic letter asking for the return of an item.*

# Notice to Builder of Defect

[*Date*]

_____

_____

_____

Dear _____ :

[*Mr. and Mrs. Riley*], who purchased your [*Glenway*] home through our office, have informed us that [*the roof leaks in five places*]. They are very concerned about this matter. It would be greatly appreciated if this deficiency were promptly corrected. Small matters often become major problems if not taken care of quickly. More important, an unhappy buyer can reflect on both of our reputations.

I look forward to continued beneficial cooperation between our firms and continued success in selling your homes.

Yours truly,

_____

**NOTE:** *This letter sells the benefits of solving the problem.*

# After-Closing Thank-You—Buyer or Seller

[*Date*]

_____

_____

_____

Dear _____ :

I would like to thank you for letting me serve you in the [*sale of*] [*purchase of*] your home. [*I am certain your new home will bring your family much happiness.*] [Based on the current market, I believe it was a very advantageous sale.]

If in the future I can be of any service to you in meeting your real estate needs, do not hesitate to contact me. If you are happy with my services, I hope you will recommend me to your friends.

Best wishes,

_____

# Notification to Seller of Referral

[*Date*]

_____

_____

_____

Dear _____ :

I am delighted we were able to find a buyer for your home, but I am sad you will be leaving our community. One of the problems in real estate sales is that you really get to like people and then they are gone. However, I wish you great happiness in [*Richmond*].

In order to help you meet your housing needs, I have contacted [*Tom Smith*] of [*Smith Realty*] in [*Richmond*]. [*Tom*] will be contacting you in a few days to go over your special housing needs. In this way, [*he*] can have a group of homes ready for you to check out when you arrive. I have also contacted the [*Richmond*] Chamber of Commerce, and they will be sending you area information and maps.

If ever I can again be of service to you, please don't hesitate to contact me.

Your friend,

_____

# Chapter

## 6

# Owner Cancellation/ Breach of Listing

# Demand for Commission—
# Owner Removes Property from Market

[*Date*]

_____

_____

_____

Dear _____ :

In accordance with an exclusive agency contract dated
_____ , [*Clyde Realty*] has been using diligence in
order to obtain a buyer for your property at _____ .

On [_____ ], before the expiration of the agency
contract, you [*informed this office that the property was
no longer available for sale*]. In accordance with the
terms of the contract, demand is hereby made for
$_____ , which is [*6% of the list price, the amount
specified as damages should you remove the property
from the market or otherwise make it unmarketable
prior to the expiration of our agency agreement*].

If you have any questions, please contact me by
[_____ ].

Sincerely,


_____

**111**

# Response to Owner or Attorney—
## Cancellation of Listing

[*Date*]

_____
_____
_____

Dear _____ :

I am in receipt of your letter of _____ , in which you are unilaterally canceling the listing agreement of _____ on the property located at _____ .

[*We have diligently worked toward the sale of said property and have been fully meeting our contractual obligations. Therefore, in accordance with the terms of the listing, demand is hereby made for $—— as commission owed based on the breach of the contract in canceling the exclusive right-to-sell agency agreement*].

[*While we have worked diligently toward the sale of the property, we do understand the unique circumstances involved and are willing to meet with you in the hopes of reaching a mutually satisfactory settlement*].

Yours truly,

_____

# Property Taken off Market
# Without Commission

[*Date*]

_____

_____

_____

Dear _____ :

In accordance with your request, we will no longer
advertise or show your [*home*] at _____ for sale.
We will also take down our sign and remove the property
from our multiple listing service.

The listing, however, will remain in full force and effect. If
you or anyone else sells the [*house*] while our agreement
is in effect, we will of course expect our full compensation
in accordance with the terms of our exclusive right-to-sell
listing.

Should you later decide to sell your home, we hope you
will consider the services and courtesy we have shown
you.

Yours truly,

_____

**NOTE:** *This is not a release. A release from the listing would allow
the owner to sell without paying any commission. This
offers protection against the owner asking to be released
with the intention of saving a commission because he or
she has secretly located a buyer.*

**113**

# Demand for Commission—
## Owner's Action Prevents Sale

[Date]

_____

_____

_____

Dear _____ :

Pursuant to our [exclusive agency listing agreement] as to your property at _____ , our office was successful in obtaining an offer on said property. You accepted this offer to purchase on [ _____ ].

A sale was not concluded because you [were unable to clear title] [failed to comply with the condition that the roof be replaced] [refused to complete the transaction].

Since our office has fully complied with the terms of said listing agreement in obtaining a buyer who was ready, willing and able to buy under price and terms agreed to by you, demand is hereby made for a commission of $ _____ based on the purchase price of $_____ .

If you have any questions, please contact me by [ _____ ].

Yours truly,


_____


**NOTE:** _The date to contact you provides a hint of dire consequences if the owner fails to do so._

114

# Demand for Commission—
# Owner Refuses Full-Price Offer

[*Date*]

_____

_____

_____

Dear _____ :

Under the terms of our exclusive listing agreement dated
_____ , [*Clyde Realty*] worked diligently to obtain a
buyer for your property at _____.

On [*August 1, 1990*], we presented you with a full-price
offer of $_____ in full accordance with the terms
specified in the listing agreement. The buyer, [*Jane Jones*],
was ready, willing and able to complete the purchase.

Your response to said offer was to [*refuse to sell*] [*counter
the offer with a price greater than the listing provided
for*] [*demand cash when the listing agreement provided
for you to carry back a $50,000 second mortgage*].

Because the sale was prevented due to your refusal to sell
in accordance with the terms of our agency agreement,
demand is hereby made for a commission of $_____
in accordance with paragraph _____ of said agreement.

If you have any questions, please contact me by [August 15].

Yours truly,


_____


**NOTE:** *By setting a date, you force the recipient to consider his or
her options. While a letter puts the demand on record, a personal contact should be made to try to resolve the problem.*

# Chapter

# 7

# Residential Buyer Solicitation

# Tired of Renting?

**Tired of Renting?**

- Would you like the privacy of a home?
- Would you like affordable home payments?
- Would you like home equity rather than rent receipts?

If you want to find out how you can be an owner rather than a renter with a down payment and monthly payments tailored to your individual needs, call me immediately at [*555-8200*].

[*Jim James*]
[*Clyde Realty*]

# Escape the Landlord

### Escape the Landlord

If you're tired of collecting rent receipts and would like to have something for your money, call me today. I have homes with:

- Low-low and even no down payments
- Monthly payments that seem like rent

[*Tom Jones*]
[*Associate Broker*]
[*Clyde Realty*]                              [*555-8200*]

# Love Your Landlord?

### Love Your Landlord?

I bet your landlord loves you. Your landlord gets the rent and tax deductions and you get rent receipts. That's a pretty good deal—for your landlord.

### Kiss Your Landlord Goodbye

If you qualify, we can put you in a house with no down payment. We also can help you arrange low-down-payment FHA financing. Call today and let us show you how your monthly payments can be building equity for you.

[*Tom Hendricks*]
[*Sales Associate*]
[*Clyde Realty*]                    [*555-8200*]

# Tenant Solicitation

[*Date*]

_____

_____

_____

Dear _____ :

Before we advertise to the general public, we would like to give you the first opportunity to purchase your home at _____ which has just been placed on the market.

I will be calling you in the next few days to provide any information you may desire and to discuss various financing arrangements that are possible.

Yours truly,


_____


**NOTE:** *This letter gives very little information, but makes the tenant think of the possibility of becoming an owner and of the forthcoming call.*

# Tenant Solicitation—Condominium Conversion

[*Date*]

_____

_____

_____

Dear _____ :

As you may be aware, [*John Jones*], the owner of your apartment building, [*is in the process of converting your building to condominiums*] [*has received approval for the conversion of your building to cooperatives*]. Our office will be handling the sale of the units.

As the tenant, you have the first opportunity to purchase your unit, which will be available at [*$187,500*]. If you are interested, I would be happy to show you the various financing options available, as well as to explain purchase terms. Please call me if you desire any information.

Yours truly,

_____

# Offer To Aid in Tenant Relocation

[*Date*]

_____

_____

_____

Dear _____ :

I would like to offer my services to help you in meeting your relocation housing needs as to rental or home purchase. Please contact me so we can discuss finding you a new home.

Yours truly,


_____


**NOTE:** *This letter could be used where apartments are converted to cooperatives or condominiums or where property is taken by eminent domain or being razed for redevelopment.*

# New Parents

[*Date*]

_____

_____

_____

Dear _____ :

Congratulations on your new [son] [daughter].

While I won't help out with the 2:00 A.M. feeding or the diapers, I can help you if you need more family space.

We have an unusually good selection of family homes, many of which offer flexible financing to meet individual buyer needs.

If you want to know more, call me today at [*555-8200*].

Yours truly,

_____

**NOTE:** *Birth announcements in newspapers are particularly effective when you can tell from the address whether the family is living in an apartment, condominium or mobile home.*

**125**

# Marriage or Engagement

[*Date*]

_____

_____

_____

Dear _____ :

Congratulations on your recent [*marriage*] [*engagement*].

I would like to offer my assistance in meeting any present or future housing needs. We have rentals ranging from $ _____ to $_____ per month and homes that can be purchased with down payments and financing tailored to your particular needs.

For a housing consultation without cost or obligation, please give me a call today at [*555-8200*].

Yours truly,


_____

# Open House Visitor

[Date]

_____

_____

_____

Dear _____ :

I would like to thank you for visiting our firm's open house at _____ this [past weekend].

I will be calling you in the next few days to ask your impression of the house and how it fits your needs. I have also enclosed information on several other homes we have available. If you are interested in any of them, I will be happy to arrange a showing.

Yours truly,


_____

Enclosures

---

**NOTE:** *A letter saying you will call forces a person to think about the call and what they will tell you. It is a power approach to letter-writing.*

# Notice to Open House Visitor of Sale

[*Date*]

_____

_____

_____

Dear _____ :

The open house you recently viewed at _____ has just been sold. We have, however, recently received several very attractive new listings that I feel will be of great interest to you.

I feel certain I can find the perfect home for you as to size, location, price and terms. Call me today so I can begin to work for you immediately.

Yours truly,


_____


**NOTE:** *A more effective last sentence might be: "I will be contacting you in the next few days to ascertain your specific housing needs."*

# Property Inquiry Letter #1

[*Date*]

_____

_____

_____

Dear _____ :

The [*111 Midvale Lane*] property that you have inquired about offers what I regard as a very special opportunity. While you really must see the property in person to fully appreciate it, I have enclosed a descriptive sheet for you.

I will call you in the next few days to answer any questions you may have as well as to tell you about several other properties that should be of interest to you.

Yours truly,


_____


**NOTE:** *The purpose of the call would be to set up a definite time to show the property.*

# Property Inquiry Letter #2

[*Date*]

_____

_____

_____

Dear _____ :

I am very happy to send you the material requested on the [*30 acres and 2 houses*] advertised in the [*Sunday Daily Ledger*].

I have also included information on several similar properties that are available. I will call you in a few days so we can arrange for you to view what I regard as a rare opportunity.

Yours truly,

_____

Enclosures

# Chamber of Commerce Inquiry

[*Date*]

_____

_____

_____

Dear _____ :

The [*Midvale*] Chamber of Commerce has indicated you are considering becoming one of our neighbors.

While perhaps being a bit premature, I would like to welcome you to our community and offer you our re-location assistance. I would be happy to arrange motel reservations when you visit the area. If you desire any specific information, let me know.

Included is some general information about several of our housing opportunities. I will call you in a few days to ascertain your specific needs.

Yours truly,


_____


**NOTE:** *You might wish to include the Housing Needs Checklist on page 133 with this letter. Then, instead of the last sentence of the letter, the following could be inserted: "I have also enclosed a Housing Needs Checklist which will help me in meeting your specific needs. I will call you in the next few days to find out when I can show you our community and the many fine homes we are offering."*

# Person Contemplating Moving to the Area

[*Date*]

_____

_____

_____

Dear _____ :

[*XYZ, Inc.*,] informed us you may be moving to our community. I would like to offer my services to you in order to meet your housing needs. I have included information on several of the properties currently available; however, if you would fill out the enclosed checklist, I will prepare housing information specific to your particular needs.

Yours truly,


_____

Enclosure

---

**NOTE:** *Sources of information of people moving to your area could come from Chamber of Commerce inquiries, inquiries to school districts, personnel offices of local firms, etc. Include a postage-paid addressed envelope.*

# Housing Needs Checklist

## Clyde Realty—Housing Checklist

Presently I own a home _____        rent _____
Must you sell before you relocate? _____
Is your home currently on the market? _____
Which do you prefer?
        to rent _____        to purchase _____
Estimated rental range  $_____   – $ _____
Estimated purchase price

    _____ Under $60,000
    _____ $60,000–$80,000
    _____ $80,000–$100,000
    _____ $100,000–$125,000
    _____ $125,000–$150,000
    _____ $150,000–$200,000
    _____ Over $200,000

Size of family:
Names and ages of children _____ , \_\_\_\_ ;
_____ , \_\_\_\_ ; _____ , \_\_\_\_ .
Number of bedrooms required _____
Number of baths required        _____
Particular locations I am interested in (if known): _____
_____ .
Required special features: _____
_____ .
Desired special features: _____
_____ .
I expect to be:
    Checking the area around: _____
    Relocating by: _____

Name: _____
Address: _____
Phone: _____

**NOTE:** *This checklist can be used as an enclosure with the answer to any inquiry about property.*

# Chapter

# 8

# Business and Investment Buyer Solicitation

# Builder Solicitation—Lots

[*Date*]

_____

_____

_____

Dear _____ :

We have recently listed [*20*] lots in [*Midvale Heights*]. The lots all have [*sewer and water in and paid for*], and are competitively priced from [*$ 27,500 to $ 31,500, with terms possible*].

I will call you in the next few days to discuss a convenient time to show you these desirable building sites.

Yours truly,


_____


**NOTE:** *The letter takes for granted the reader's interest, and the mention of a phone call forces the reader to give a few seconds to the idea of lots in the area specified. The phone call should offer the choice of time of showing, not ask whether the builder wants a showing.*

# Adjoining Owner Solicitation

[*Date*]

_____

_____

_____

Dear _____ :

We have just listed the property at [ *111 Midvale Lane* ] for sale. Since this property adjoins your land, we felt you should have the first opportunity to purchase it. We are, therefore, notifying you prior to advertising to the general public.

I am certain you understand the advantage of owning this adjoining parcel. Please call me so I can provide you with specific information.

Yours truly,

_____

**NOTE:** *This letter is a teaser. It creates urgency and a desire. It can be used for raw land, lots, farms and even income or investment property. A great many properties are sold to adjoining property owners.*

# Owner of Similar Investment Property in Area

[*Date*]

_____

_____

_____

Dear _____ :

When we listed the [*24-unit apartment building at 3305–3307 Chestnut Boulevard*], I immediately thought this would be the ideal investment for the owner of the property at [*3309 Chestnut Boulevard*].

Because the property [*is right next door to your property*] [*is so close to your property and is so similar*], the management advantages of dual ownership are readily apparent.

The property is available at [*an attractive price with flexible terms*][*$1.5 million with approximately $150,000 down*] [*a price and terms that will allow an immediate positive cash flow*]. I will be calling you in the next few days to discuss the advantages this fine property can offer you.

Yours truly,

_____

P.S.: If you are not interested in purchasing this property, perhaps you would consider selling your property. The advantages to a buyer owning both properties could make for an exceptional sale opportunity.

**NOTE:** *The P.S. raises the interesting switch that if the reader isn't a buyer, then he or she should be a seller. It also reinforces the advantages of owning the two properties.*

# Tenant Solicitation of Ownership

[Date]

_____

_____

_____

Dear _____ :

How would you like your office to be in [Perkins Plaza]
[the Perkins Building]* and not have to move?

Your present [office building] [commercial building]
has just been placed on the market. It offers you a rare
opportunity. You can be your own landlord and be entitled
to depreciation, income and appreciation instead of only a
growing pile of rent receipts.

Call me today to discuss the possibility of making [Perkins
Plaza] a reality.

Yours truly,


_____

*Use tenant's name here.

**NOTE:** *This letter should be sent to professional tenants and strong
retail tenants. It has an excellent approach to pride by
giving the building the name of the buyer being solicited.*

# Tenant Solicitation—Office Condominium

[*Date*]

_____

_____

_____

Dear _____ :

Did you realize you could move your office less than
[*3 blocks*] and have

- Absolute protection against future rent increases
- The tax advantage of depreciation
- Payments that increase your equity rather than
  worthless rent receipts
- An investment that will likely show exceptional
  appreciation
- A hedge against inflation

We have several outstanding office condominiums for sale
that offer you advantages that a rental cannot provide,
and are bound to please your accountant. We should be
able to make you an owner with little or no increase in
actual monthly costs and a down payment tailored to
your needs.

While this may sound too good to be true, I will prove to
you and your accountant everything I said is true. If you
don't want to say, "I should have . . . ," call me immediately.

Yours truly,


_____


**NOTE:** *By canvassing the buildings close to your listing or by
using a reverse directory, you can put together a sizable
mailing list.*

# Franchise—General Needs

[*Date*]

_____

_____

_____

Attention: Real Estate Officer

I would like to be your real estate eyes and ears in [*Clark and Humboldt Counties*].

If you would let me know your real estate needs as to size, traffic count, access, price, etc., I would be happy to put my area knowledge to work for you.

Yours truly,

_____

**NOTE:** *Names and addresses of franchises are available from franchise magazines, as well as from several books on franchises. The research librarian at your local public library can help you locate these.*

# Franchise—Specific Location

[*Date*]

_____

_____

_____

Dear _____ :

Our office has recently listed [*a property at 55 Chestnut Boulevard*]. Because of [*access and traffic*], I feel it would be an excellent location for one of your franchises. The parcel is [*200 feet x 100 feet*]. An attractive [*purchase price*] [*lease*] is available. Please let me know as to your interest.

I am willing to work with you in meeting your real estate needs within [*Dade County*]. If you could let me know your specific interests, my eyes and ears are available for you.

Yours truly,

_____

**NOTE:** *Names and addresses of franchises are available from franchise magazines as well as from several books on franchises. The research librarian at your local public library can help you locate these.*

# White Elephant Investment

---

### What To Do with a White Elephant?

We are looking for an investor with vision who can come up with a productive use for:

[*a seven-story, 74,000-square-foot former textile plant on a three-acre site north of Highway 30 with rail siding.*]

Sure it's a problem, but the price of [*$690,000*] reflects the problem. If you have the solution you have an exceptional opportunity. Call me today for a private showing. Let's see how sharp you really are!

[*Tom Sharpe*]
[*Clyde Realty*]                              [*555-8200*]

---

**NOTE:** *This is an excellent flier for owners of property in the area, creative investors and developers.*

# Safe Investment

### Want A Safe Investment?
### [*Insured Lease?*]
### [*Insurable Lease?*]

Would you like monotonous rent checks, month after month, year after year [*and the tenant pays the taxes and makes the repairs*]?

If a risk-free, care-free investment interests you and you can handle a [*$250,000*] down payment, call me to learn the advantages this fine investment property has to offer.

[*Sylvia Sharpe*]
[*Clyde Realty*]                                    [*555-8200*]

**NOTE:** *As written, this solicitation is for a triple-net property leased to a strong tenant, making rent insurance possible.*

# $100,000 Investment

### Better than a Jumbo CD

We have a safe real estate investment that offers

- A hedge against inflation
- Leverage opportunities
- Appreciation
- Professional management

Plus, income comparable to CDs. Except our income is going to be tax-free.

If you want more information what a [*$100,000*] investment can mean to your security, call me today for information on this exceptional opportunity.

[*Joe Jones*]
[*Clyde Realty*]                                   [*555-8200*]

**NOTE:** *Income will be tax-free because it is sheltered by depreciation. Jumbo certificates of deposit (CDs) are in $100,000 denominations.*

# Referral Investor

[*Date*]

_____

_____

_____

Dear _____ :

[*Alice Smith*] recommended I contact you. We have just listed an exceptional investment opportunity that [*she*] thought might interest you.

It is a [*low-risk property*] offering the [*possibility of extraordinary appreciation coupled with tax-sheltered income*]. It would require a down payment of around [*$110,000*].

If you are interested in safeguarding your future, please give me a call today.

Yours truly,

_____

**NOTE:** *This letter gives very little detail other than amount of down payment. It is aimed at getting the addressee to call you so you can qualify him or her as to specific needs. While a real property should be used, it is used to tantalize. Details increase the likelihood of including what might appear negative to the recipient.*

# Syndicate Formation

[*Date*]

_____

_____

_____

Dear _____ :

I am putting together a small group of local investors to take part in an exceptional investment opportunity as limited partners. [*Joe Jones has recommended you as a person who would appreciate taking part in this opportunity.*] [*You indicated some time ago that I should contact you if a really great opportunity presented itself.*]

Since you have seen the appreciation of the past few years, you will understand the desirability of this prime low-risk real estate project.

Investors must be able to make a [*$20,000*] minimum investment. If you would like more details, I am having an informal meeting of potential investors at my home at [*1744 Midvale Lane*] [*Saturday morning, April 10th at 10 A.M.*]. After I have discussed the opportunity and answered your questions, those who are interested will have an opportunity to visit the property involved.

If you are interested in attending the [*Saturday morning*] meeting, please let me know as soon as possible, as the number of investors is limited.

Yours truly,

_____

===========================================================

**NOTE:** *A morning home meeting provides a nonthreatening atmosphere. Also, the fact that it is a group meeting tends to reduce apprehension. For a syndicate solicitation, be certain you have checked your state laws. Syndicate agreements should be prepared by an attorney.*

# Operating Income and Expenses

[*Date*]

Dear _____ :

The following is a statement of income and expenses for the property located at _____ . The figures set forth are based on [*a copy of the latest tax return provided by the owner*] [*a statement provided by the owner*] [*the books provided us by the owner*] [*the property management statements*].

| | |
|---|---|
| Scheduled gross annual income | $ _____ |
| Vacancy and collection loss | $ _____ |
| Adjusted gross annual income | $ _____ |
| | |
| Taxes [*1989*] | $ _____ |
| Insurance cost [*1989*] | $ _____ |
|   Policy provider [*Jones Underwriters*] | |
| Utilities [*Based on last 12 months*] | $ _____ |
| Management costs [*last 12 months*] | $ _____ |
| Maintenance and repair [*1989*] | $ _____ |
| Miscellaneous expenses [*1989*] | $ _____ |
|   Total expenses | $ _____ |
|   [*before debt service*] | |
| | |
|   Net operating income | $ _____ |
| [*not considering debt service*] | |

It should be pointed out that just a 10 percent increase in rents would increase the net income by $ _____ and rentals have been experiencing an annual increase of approximately _____ per cent per year. Carrying this past increase forward for five years would mean an increase of $_____ in rent, most of which would be reflected in the net.

If you have any further questions, please do not hesitate to contact me.

_____

# Notice to Business Owner
# of Related Business for Sale

[*Date*]

_____

_____

_____

Dear _____ :

Because you are in the [*retail hardware*] business, you now have an exceptional opportunity for expansion.

We have just listed for sale a [*successful hardware store*] that offers great potential. The books are open to you and your accountant. Call me at once for more details as this is an opportunity deserving of your immediate attention.

Yours truly,

_____

**NOTE:** *This letter is a teaser to excite interest. Very little information should be given as to the business and it should not be identified at this time.*

# Supplier or Wholesaler—
# Business Opportunity

[*Date*]
_____
_____
_____

Dear _____ :

Because you are a [*hardware distributor*] [*hardware wholesaler*], I thought you should be aware of the [*retail hardware store*] we recently listed for sale. It is located at [*105 Midvale*] and the price of $_____ includes [*all fixtures and an advantageous lease*]. The books are open to a qualified buyer [*and owner financing is possible*].

If any of your customers are interested in an exceptional expansion opportunity, please have them contact me.

Yours truly,


_____


**NOTE:** *Suppliers have a stake in finding a buyer, as it can create an obligation. A great many businesses are sold to buyers based on information gained from suppliers.*

*For a supplier letter, the business must be identified and a price or price range should be included.*

# Chapter

# 9

# Buyer Letters

# Prospective Buyer—New Listing

[*Date*]

_____

_____

_____

Dear _____ :

[*I was unable to reach you by phone.*] We have just taken a new listing, which I feel is exactly what you have been looking for. I want you to see this very special home before it is advertised to the general public.

Please call me at once, as I wouldn't want you to miss this opportunity.

Yours truly,

_____

**NOTE:** *Send this letter special delivery.*

*This letter creates an urgency and sets a buying rather than looking mood. No information is given because if it included anything buyers considered negative, they would not be eager to see the property.*

*You can continue the urgency mood by asking prospective buyers whether they can take off work to see it. If they like the house, they will be happy they did.*

**Warning:** *Be reasonably certain this is the house for your clients, or your credibility could be damaged.*

# Prospective Buyer—Price Reduction

[*Date*]

_____

_____

_____

Dear _____ :

The house you liked so much in [*Elmside*], the one with
[*the huge fireplace and the fruit trees in the backyard*]
has just been reduced in price. The original price set by
the owners was [*$169,500*], but they have reduced this
to [*$150,000*], a net reduction of [*$19,500*].

This reduction should result in a very quick sale. Because
I would hate to see anyone else get this exceptional buy, I
think you should take another look at this property. I will
be calling you to arrange a showing of this home and
another new listing I think will interest you.

Yours truly,

_____

**NOTE:** *While an initial phone call would normally be superior to
a letter, this letter would be appropriate to a prospective
buyer living outside the area. The letter would be proper
if the prospects indicated mild interest.*

*The mention of the other home is a final hook to set up the
showings.*

# Offer to Buyer

[*Date*]

_____

_____

_____

Dear _____ :

In accordance with our [*telephone discussion on Wednesday, October 8th*], I have prepared an offer to purchase for the property at [*111 Midvale Lane*]. The offer reflects your offering price of [*$165,000*] as well as [*include terms, etc., that vary from the listing as well as any special conditions*].

Please sign and return [*two*] copies of the purchase agreement to me as soon as possible as well as [*your deposit check for $16,500*], which will be [*held uncashed until the offer is accepted*]. In the event the offer is not accepted, your deposit will be returned to you in full.

If your offer is accepted by the owners, I believe you will have made an exceptionally fine purchase. Even at the list price I think this home is an excellent buy.

Yours truly,

_____

Enclosure

**NOTE:** *The last sentence really sets the buyer toward looking favorably at a counteroffer.*

# Acceptance to Buyer

[*Date*]

_____

_____

_____

Dear _____ :

Enclosed is a signed acceptance of your offer to purchase
the property at [*55 Chestnut Street*].

I will be contacting you in a few days to go over requirements for closing and to provide advice and assistance
as needed.

You have purchased a [*home*] that I believe will provide
you with much happiness.

Yours truly,

_____

Enclosure

# Rejection of Offer—No Counteroffer

[*Date*]

_____

_____

_____

Dear _____ :

[*Mr. and Mrs. Jones*] have indicated they are unable to accept your offer to purchase their home.

While they would very much like to sell to you, they feel the price they had set is more than reasonable based on the current real estate marketplace.

Because I feel very strongly that this home meets your needs better than any other home available and that the price asked is favorable, I have enclosed a new offer form reflecting that price.

If you wish to be the owner of this fine home, please sign and return [*two*] copies of the offer in the envelope provided. [*It would be unfortunate to lose this fine opportunity for a difference of only about 5%.*]

Yours truly,

_____

P.S.: Keep in mind that long after the price has been forgotten you will be enjoying the amenities of this fine home.

**NOTE:** *If at all possible, buyers should be immediately notified by phone or in person of rejection of their offer. If a phone contact was made, start the letter with, "In accordance with our telephone discussion. . . "*

# Counteroffer

[Date]

_____

_____

_____

Dear _____ :

The owners [Mr. and Mrs. Smith], were unable to accept your offer of [$90,000] for their property at [55 Crescent Cove]. [They feel they would be receiving far less than would be necessary to obtain replacement housing.] [They feel they cannot take a loss of that magnitude.] [While they like you and would like you as the new owners, they are just unable to accept your offer.]

They have made you what I regard as an extremely attractive counteroffer, which would allow you to obtain an exceptional purchase. You will see they have lowered their price [$20,000]. If you sign and return [two] copies to our office, you will be the owner of a home you can truly be proud of at a price that is far less than I thought possible.

Yours truly,


_____

Enclosure

---

**NOTE:** _If you are preparing a counteroffer to be presented by mail, it is suggested that a new form be used so that the buyers need only sign, rather than initial and date changes. The sellers should sign and the places for buyer signatures should be checked with red ink._

# Buyer Cost Estimate

[*Date*]

_____

_____

_____

Dear _____ :

Enclosed is our Buyer Cost Estimation Work Sheet.

While we believe the estimates are reasonably reliable, they are not guaranteed.

If you have any questions, please contact me.

Yours truly,


_____

Enclosure


**NOTE:** *The "Buyer Cost Estimation Work Sheet" is on page 164.*

# Buyer Cost Estimation Work Sheet

Buyer cost estimate for purchase of:

_____

_____

_____

| Costs | | Credits | |
|---|---|---|---|
| Purchase price: | $____ | Down payment: | $____ |
| Loan costs: | | Loans being | |
|   Appraisal fee | $____ |   assumed | $____ |
|   Origination costs | $____ | Seller financing | $____ |
|   Miscellaneous fees | $____ | Taxes (prorated) | $____ |
|   Impound account | $____ | Total credits | $____ |
| Insurance | $____ | | |
| Taxes (prorated) | $____ | | |
| Title insurance/ | | | |
|   abstracts | $____ | | |
| Attorney fees/ | | | |
|   escrow | $____ | | |
| Miscellaneous costs | $____ | | |
|    Total costs | $____ | | |

         − ____ (credits)

         $____ To be financed or paid
at closing

# Contingent Offeror Notice

[*Date*]

_____
_____
_____

Dear _____ :

Your offer-to-purchase agreement dated _____ was contingent on [_____
_____ ].

The purchase contract provides that should a subsequent written offer be accepted which is contingent on your rights, you shall have [*seven days*] to waive the contingencies set forth in your offer. You are hereby notified that a subsequent offer has been received and accepted. Unless the seller shall have received notice by _____ , that you have waived your contingencies, your offer shall terminate and become void and your earnest money deposit shall be returned to you. You are also notified that time shall be of the essence as to such notification.

If you have any questions, please contact me immediately.

Yours truly,

_____

Enclosure

*NOTE:* *Include a contingency release with this letter.*

*It is suggested that this notice be sent registered mail with a return receipt requested.*

# Problem with Contract Condition—
## Buyer or Seller

[Date]

_____

_____

_____

Dear _____ :

Your purchase contract for the [purchase] [sale] of
[ _____ ] requires that [ _____ ] be [obtained]
[completed] by [August 1].

It is my understanding the above condition has not yet
been fulfilled. You therefore are at risk of the [buyer]
[seller] declaring you to be in default of your agreement
[which could result in damages].

If there is any problem fulfilling the required condition,
please contact me immediately so I can work with you
toward a satisfactory solution.

Yours truly,

_____

**NOTE:** _A letter should only be used in this case if personal contact
is not possible. If there appears to be a problem, the other
party should of course be notified._

166

# Buyer Failed Contingency

[*Date*]

Dear _____ :

Your offer dated [*June 1, 1990*] to purchase the property at [*2736 Wright Road in Newton Heights*] was contingent on [*your obtaining a $100,000 loan with $10,000 down by July 15*]. You have been unable to [*obtain the required financing and have indicated you are unable to waive the contingency*]. Therefore, in accordance with your purchase offer, your offer has become null and void. With the concurrence of the owners, I am enclosing [*Clyde Realty*] trust account check No. [*2933*] in the amount of [*$5,000*], representing the full return of your earnest money deposit made with your offer to purchase.

If you have any questions or there is any way [*Clyde Realty*] can serve you, please contact our office.

Yours truly,

_____

Enclosure

cc: [*James C. Smith*]*

*The owner's name

# Information to New Owner

[*Date*]

_____

_____

_____

Dear _____ :

To aid you in getting established in your new home we have included a list of phone numbers for utility hook-ups, [ _____ ] as well as some general area information we feel will be useful to you. If there is anything [ *Clyde Realty* ] can do to be of further assistance, don't hesitate to call me.

Yours truly,

_____

***NOTE:*** *In addition to phone numbers, consider area maps, school information, information on religious groups, bus information, etc. Your local chamber of commerce office can likely supply you with quite a bit of information for the new resident.*

# Information on Utilities and Services

[*Date*]

_____

_____

_____

Dear _____ :

Just a few numbers that will help you in moving into your new home:

| | |
|---|---|
| *Telephone service* | _____ |
| *Gas connection* | _____ |
| *Electrical service* | _____ |
| *Water* | _____ |
| *Cable TV* | _____ |
| *Newspaper* | _____ |
| *Trash service* | _____ |
| *School registration* | |
| *[Central District]* | _____ |
| Emergency Numbers | |
| Fire | _____ |
| Police | _____ |
| Ambulance | _____ |

If you like, I would be happy to give you my recommendations for everything from an auto mechanic to a [*beauty shop*] [*barber shop*].

Sincerely,


_____

# School Registration Information

[*Date*]

_____

_____

_____

Dear _____ :

Just a quick note to let you know you [*can now register Judy and Bobby*] for [*Midvale School starting July 10th*].

By registering early, you will avoid having to rush after you move in to your new home. I am certain you will find plenty of other things to keep you busy.

Best regards,

_____

# Insurance Solicitation #1

[Date]

_____

_____

_____

Dear _____ :

Now that you are about to become the owner of a home you can be proud of, you should give some thought to your insurance. I would suggest you consider a home-owner policy in the amount of [$75,000] (remember, the land doesn't need protection), having personal liability protection of [$100,000]. This policy covers theft, vehicle damage to structure, vandalism, fire, windstorm and lightning. I would recommend replacement coverage so that in the event of a loss you would receive your actual replacement costs and not the depreciated value.

You can either contact your own agent to make certain you are covered as of [June 1, 1990], the date of closing, or if you like our office can write the policy with [United Casualty]. The annual premium for a one-year policy as recommended above would be [$430, payable in two installments]. [Enclosed is a brochure of the coverage suggested.] Let me know if you want us to handle the insurance.

Yours truly,

_____

Enclosure

# Insurance Solicitation #2

[*Date*]

_____

_____

_____

Dear _____ :

The lender [*Midvale Savings and Loan*] will be requiring
you to carry a fire policy on your new home in the
amount of at least [*$100,000*]. We recommend you
consider a home-owner's policy in the amount of
$_____ which would provide $_____ in
liability coverage as well as insure the contents to
$_____ . We also recommend replacement coverage
that pays the full value of personal property, not just a
depreciated value. Such coverage is available through your
full-service insurance agent or, if you like, we can write
the policy through our office and supply a copy to the
lender. A policy providing the coverage we have recommended would cost [*$430 for one year*] if written through
our office.

Please let me know if I can be of service to you.

Yours truly,


_____

# Insurance Solicitation—Mortgage Insurance

[*Date*]

_____

_____

_____

Dear _____ :

I hope you and your family are enjoying your lovely new home. You might be interested in the enclosed brochure. It concerns a mortgage insurance policy that will pay off your mortgage should you die, or make the payments for you should you become disabled. Because of the concern you have for your family, please give some consideration to this plan.

The premiums on your current mortgage at your age of [*39*] come to only [*$50*] per [*month*], and the payments are guaranteed to remain the same for the life of the loan.

If you are interested or have any questions, please give me a call.

Sincerely,

_____

Enclosure

---

**NOTE:** *If you wish to sell mortgage insurance, after the sale has been made is maybe the best time to contact the owners. Before the sale they are concerned about all the expenses of closing, and are more reluctant to take on new debt. Mortgage insurance is really decreasing term life insurance.*

# Buyer Breach of Purchase Agreement

[*Date*]

_____

_____

_____

Dear _____ :

According to your purchase agreement with [*Mrs. James Smith*] dated [*June 1, 1990*], for the purchase of [*555 Midvale Court*], you were required to [*increase your deposit by $10,000*] no later than [*August 3, 1990*].

You have failed to meet your contractual obligation. Therefore, I have been authorized as the agent for [*Mrs. James Smith*] to inform you that your failure is a material breach of your agreement. The seller hereby declares the above contract to be null and void based on said breach.

[*In accordance with said agreement your deposit is, therefore, forfeited as liquidated damages.*] [*The sellers reserve the right to bring legal action against you for damages suffered resulting from your breach of contract.*]

Yours truly,

_____

[*cc: Mrs. James Smith*]

**NOTE:** *Do not send this letter without specific written authorization from the owners. Also check with your legal representative, as rights vary among states.*

# Notice of Settlement Conference #1

[*Date*]

_____

_____

_____

Dear _____ :

The settlement conference for your [*sale*] [*purchase*] of [*111 Midvale Lane*] has been scheduled for [*June 1, 1990*] at [*55 Sycamore Place, Suite 3301*].

[*It is necessary that all buyers be in attendance so they can sign the mortgage.*]

[*Please have a cashier's check in the amount of $39,528.*] [*See enclosed statement.*]

I am glad we have been able to fulfill your needs.

Yours truly,


_____

Enclosure

# Notice of Settlement Conference #2

[*Date*]

_____

_____

_____

Dear _____ :

I have enclosed a statement showing total closing costs, [*loans*] and the balance due at closing for your new home at [*111 Crescent Cove*].

Please bring a cashier's check in the amount of [*$39,528*] to the closing, made out to *James Smith*. The closing is scheduled for [*10 A.M.*] on [*Wednesday, April 3rd*], at [*3301 Sycamore Boulevard*].

Yours truly,

_____

Enclosure

# Closing Statement Transmittal

[*Date*]

_____

_____

_____

Dear _____ :

Enclosed is a copy of the closing statement for your purchase of [*6160 Jupiter Lane*].

[*I am certain you will have many happy years in your new home.*] If in the future you or your friends have any real estate needs, I hope you will think of me.

Yours truly,


_____

Enclosure

# Notice to Apply
# for Home-Owner Tax Exemption

[*Date*]

_____

_____

_____

Dear _____ :

Our state offers a special property tax exemption for owner-occupied homes. You must, however, apply for this exemption by [*September 1*] for the 19[*90*] tax year. I have enclosed [*information on applying for the exemption*] [*an exemption application*] for your convenience.

I would hate for you not to obtain the benefits you are entitled to. If you have any questions, please contact me.

Sincerely,


_____


**NOTE:** *In many states, a resident home owner is entitled to special tax treatment, but the home owner must apply for it.*

# Buyer Purchased from Another

[Date]

_____

_____

_____

Dear _____ :

Congratulations! I was very happy to learn you had found the [home] that fulfills your needs. While I am sorry I was unable to locate that [special home] for you, I do wish you happiness in your new [home]. From what I know of the area, I am certain you made a wise choice.

If in the future you need real estate assistance, don't hesitate to contact me. I am ready to use my best efforts on your behalf.

Yours truly,

_____

**NOTE:** _This letter reestablishes the relationship for future referral calls or dealings. Otherwise, the buyers might avoid the agent who they feel is angry at them for going elsewhere._

# Anniversary of Purchase

[*Date*]

_____

_____

_____

Dear _____ :

It is hard to realize it, but we are celebrating our anniversary this week. On [*June 1*], it will be exactly [*four*] years since [*I sold you your home*] [*you purchased your home through our office*]. I hope your home has been good to you in those years; I know it has certainly appreciated in value.

If [*I*] [*we*] can be of service to you in the future as to any of your real estate needs, don't hesitate to contact me. Again, a happy anniversary.

Yours truly,

_____

**180**

# Chapter

# 10

# Property Management

# Rental Inquiry

[*Date*]

_____

_____

_____

Dear _____ :

In accordance with your inquiry we have the following units available for [*June 1st occupancy*] [*immediate occupancy*], which appear to meet your stated requirements:

[*Two-bedroom, two-bath at 1822 West Stevens, $430/ month with $400 security deposit on a one-year lease (no pets).*]

[*Two-bedroom at 731 West Third Street at $400/month with a $400 security deposit on a one-year lease.*]

I would be happy to show you either of these units when you are in town.

Yours truly,

_____

**NOTE:** *You might include this phrase, if applicable: "We also have several homes and condominiums that can be purchased with very low down payments and monthly payments within your indicated payment range."*

# Approval of Rental Application

[*Date*]

_____

_____

_____

Dear _____ :

Your rental application has been approved for [*733 West Third Street*] with occupancy of [*October 31st*].

Please come to [*our office*] by _____ to sign the lease and to pay the balance of the required deposits as follows:

| | |
|---|---|
| [Rent *October 1–31* | $ 480 ] |
| [*Last month's rent* | $ 480 ] |
| [*Security deposit* | $ 480 ] |
| Total advance rent and deposits | [ ($1,440) ] |
| less application deposit | [ ( 200 ) ] |
| Balance due: | [ ($1,240) ] |

Yours truly,

_____

# Rental Application Rejection #1

[*Date*]

_____

_____

_____

Dear _____ :

Enclosed is [*your check*] [*our check*] in the amount of
[*$200*], which constitutes the return of your rental
application for _____ [*less the nonrefundable
credit report fee of $_____* ].

We have accepted another applicant for the premises.

[*We do have several other units available in other buildings:*]

| Address | Size | Rental |
|---------|------|--------|
| [*1732 Third Street* | *2 BR 2 Bath* | *$600*] |
| [*501 Chestnut Circle* | *2 BR 1 1/2 Bath* | *$550*] |
| [*2001 Jupiter Avenue* | *2 BR 1 Bath* | *$650*] |

If you wish to view any of these units, please contact our
office.

[*We also have a number of properties for sale with reasonable or low down payments. If you should like more information on these, please contact me.*]

Thank you for considering our property and we hope you will be able to locate suitable housing.

Yours truly,

_____

**NOTE:** *By mentioning other housing opportunities, you lessen the likelihood of rental applicants feeling they were discriminated against. Of course, if the reason for rejection of the tenant was poor credit or rental history, you would not want to mention other properties.*

# Rental Application Rejection #2

[*Date*]

_____

_____

_____

Dear _____ :

We regret to inform you that your rental application for
[*2001 Jupiter Avenue*] has been rejected.

Enclosed is [*your check*] [*our check*] for [*$300*], which
represents the return of your rental deposit.

Yours truly,

_____

**NOTE:** *If a nonrefundable fee for credit application costs was
agreed to, continue the last sentence with: "less the
nonrefundable [credit report fee] of [$20] as agreed to in
your rental application."*

*It is strongly suggested you avoid reasons for rejecting
applications, as they tend to lead to protracted confronta-
tions. You should fully document your files, however, since
complaints are sometimes made by applicants claiming
wrongful bias.*

# Late Payment—Waiver of Late Charge

[*Date*]

_____

_____

_____

Dear _____ :

Your rent payment for the month of _____ was due
at our office on _____ . It was not received until
_____ .

A late charge of $_____ is authorized by paragraph
_____ of your lease.

Since this is your first late payment, we will waive the late
charge in this instance. However, it is essential that
future rent payments be received on time. Should any
future rent payment be received late, a late charge as
provided by your lease agreement will be assessed against
you.

Yours truly,


_____

# Late Payment Charge #1

[*Date*]

_____

_____

_____

Dear _____ :

Your rent payment for the month of _____ , was due at our office on _____ . It was not received until _____ .

You are hereby notified that in accordance with paragraph _____ of your lease, you have been assessed a late charge of $ _____ which is due <u>immediately</u>.

It is essential this charge, as well as any future rent payments, be paid in accordance with your lease.

Yours truly,


_____

# Late Payment Charge #2

[*Date*]

_____

_____

_____

Dear _____ :

Your rent payment due on [*August 1st*], which was received on [*August 7th*], did not include a late charge of _____ as specified in paragraph _____ of your lease.

Please remit this amount immediately.

Yours truly,

_____

# Bad Check

---

[*Date*]

_____

_____

_____

Dear _____ :

Your check no. _____ in the amount of $_____
made out to _____ has been returned to us from
your bank marked nonsufficient funds.

Please see that this office is furnished with either a
money order, cashier's check or certified check in the
amount of $ _____ by _____ . Failure to
comply shall be regarded as a breach of your legal obligations.

Yours truly,


_____

---

**NOTE:** *No threat of legal action is made, although it might be
possibly implied. A date is set to express urgency. The letter
makes clear that a personal check will not be accepted.*

*A middle paragraph could be inserted as follows:*
*"In accordance with your lease, a charge of [$ 25] has
been added to the rental due for the nonsufficient funds
check."*

# Notice of Impending Rent Increase

[*Date*]

_____

_____

_____

Dear _____ :

Because of [*increased operational costs*] [*increases in taxes*] [*improvements we have made to the property*], we are being forced to review our rent schedules. We will notify you by [*April 1st*] of any changes that might be necessary.

Yours truly,

_____

**NOTE:** *The purpose of this letter is to prepare the tenant for a modest rent increase. Since tenants will expect the worst, a reasonable increase will be met with relief rather than a negative reaction. This letter should precede the rent increase notification by no more than 10 days.*

# Rent Increase #1

[Date]

_____

_____

_____

Dear _____ :

Because of [increased expenses] [increased interest rates] [improvements we have made], a rental adjustment has become necessary.

As of [May 1], the rent for [5800 Crescent Cove, #3-S] shall be increased from the current [$600] per month to [$625] per month.

Yours truly,


_____


**NOTE:** _Be certain notices comply with your state laws as to both content and service of the notice (registered mail might be required)._

# Rent Increase #2

[*Date*]

_____

_____

_____

Dear _____ :

You are hereby notified [*in accordance with Arizona law*] that as of [*January 1, 1990*], your rent shall be increased from [*$600*] per month to [*$625*] per month for the premises at [*643 Jupiter Lane, second floor*].

Yours truly,

_____

**NOTE:** *Make certain rent increase notices are given for the statutory period. As an example, a number of states require notices at least 30 days prior to the rent increase, and in some states the notice must end on the rent paying date.*

*Consider use of registered or certified mail, and request return receipts. This avoids the claim of nondelivery or your notice being mistaken for junk mail. Your state statutes may specify the manner of delivering the notice as well as the form of the notice.*

# Complaint about Tenant's Breach of Rules

[*Date*]

_____

_____

_____

Dear _____ :

We have received a complaint as to_____

[*which has been confirmed by our resident manager*].
Such action, is of course, a violation of the occupancy
rules you signed at the time you leased the premises.

Apartment dwellers must live in proximity to others. It is
therefore necessary that each resident respect the rights
of others. Should there be further problems, it could
result in the necessity of eviction procedures in accordance with the provisions of your lease agreement.

Yours truly,


_____

# Notice to Cease Prohibited Activity

[*Date*]

_____

_____

_____

Dear _____ :

It has come to our attention that [*you have been performing major automobile repair work in your parking space at 110 Stardust Lane*].

This is a violation of [*your lease*] [*the occupancy rules and regulations you signed at the time of rental*].

You are hereby ordered to cease this activity immediately or corrective action shall be required in accordance with your lease.

Yours truly,

_____

# Notice to Tenant—Failure to Maintain Exterior or Lawns

[*Date*]

_____

_____

_____

Dear _____ :

In [*driving by*] [*inspecting*] the [*home at 12 West Davis Street*], which you are renting from our office, I was surprised to see that [*the lawn has not been cared for*].

In accordance with the terms of your lease, you are required to [*maintain the landscaping*]. Unless [*the lawn is properly maintained by August 1st*], we shall have to contract for the work with [*a gardening service*] and add the charges to your rent.

Yours truly,

_____

# Notice of Lease Automatic Renewal

[*Date*]

_____

_____

_____

Dear _____ :

Your present lease for [*the two-bedroom house*] at [*660 Stardust Circle*] expires as of [*April 1, 1990*]. This is to remind you that unless you give notice to the contrary by [*March 1, 1990*], the lease by its terms is automatically extended for [*another year*]. If you have any questions, please contact me.

Yours truly,

_____

**NOTE:** *While many owners don't remind tenants of the automatic renewal, the reminder does avoid hard feelings and later problems.*

# Lease Expiration Notice—New Lease

[*Date*]

_____

_____

_____

Dear _____ :

Your lease for [*660 Maple Lane*] will expire on [*April 1, 1990*]. I have enclosed a new lease for the premises substantially the same as your old lease except the rent has been increased to [*$625*]. The higher rent is required because of [*cost increases in the operation and management of the property*].

Please sign and return [*two*] copies of the new lease to our office by [*March 1, 1990*]. If I do not receive your new lease by this date, I will assume you do not wish to remain in possession and appropriate notices will then be given.

Yours truly,


_____

Enclosure

**NOTE:** *While it is not necessary to give reasons for a rent increase, a reason makes your action seem less arbitrary and helps to maintain better tenant relations.*

# Tenant Notice of Leaving in Violation of Lease

[*Date*]

_____

_____

_____

Dear _____ :

Your current lease, dated [*January 1, 1990*] does not
expire until [*January 1, 1991*]. If you wish to vacate the
premises before this date, you will be held liable for the
cost of re-renting the premises as well as any rental loss
incurred.

If you wish to locate a tenant to assume your lease
obligations, we will allow a lease assignment subject to
our approval based on family size, credit and previous
rental history. You, of course, would remain liable should
the new tenant default on the lease.

Please contact me immediately as to your intentions. If
you are vacating on [*September 1*], I want to start work
immediately to find a new tenant in order to keep your
legal obligations to a minimum.

Yours truly,

_____

# Tenant Vacated in Violation of Lease

[*Date*]

_____

_____

_____

Dear _____ :

I have been informed that on [*April 15*] you vacated the premises at [*1700 Sycamore Avenue*]. [*Your lease required a 30-day notice which was not given.*] [*Your lease does not expire until* _____ .] Therefore, you shall be held liable [*for the rental until the end of the lease period*] [*for the 30-day notice period expiring May 15*].

Should we be able to re-rent the premises prior to the above date, your liability will be reduced by the rent received for said period less costs of re-renting the premises.

Please contact this office immediately to make arrangements for fulfilling your obligation.

Yours truly,

_____

**NOTE:** *This letter might require modification based on state law. Contact legal counsel.*

# Notice to Vacate

[*Date*]

_____
_____
_____

Dear _____ :

In accordance with [*the terms of your tenancy*] [*Arizona law*], you are hereby notified you are ordered to vacate the premises at [*6603 Sycamore Parkway*] on or before [*May 1, 1990*]. This notice shall constitute [*30-day notice*] as required by [*state law*].

Agent for: [*Clyde Management*]

_____

**NOTE:** *Be certain of your notice requirement under your state law. Registered mail or personal service might be required. In some states the notice must end on a rent-paying date. Check with an attorney and then modify the notice if required.*

# Notice to Tenant of Damage
# on Vacating Premises

[*Date*]

_____

_____

_____

Dear _____ :

Inspection of the premises at [*6603 Sycamore, third
floor,*] that were vacated by you on [*April 1*], revealed that
[*the living room floor is scratched in several places, the
ceiling fan and miniblinds from the dining room are
missing, and the bathroom mirror is broken*]. Since the
[*damages*] [*missing articles*] [*are*] not normal wear and
tear, we have made the necessary [*repairs*] [*replace-
ments*] and have deducted the cost from your [*property
damage bond*]. (See enclosed statement.) The balance of
$75 is enclosed.

Yours truly,

_____

Enclosure

NOTE: *Alternatives to the last paragraph might be:*
   *"Since the cost of [repairs] [replacements] exceeds the
   amount of your property damage bond, please remit [$300]
   to this office no later than [4 P.M.] on [April 1]. (See
   enclosed statement.)"*

*"The necessary [repairs] [replacements] have resulted in costs of [$300]. (See enclosed statement.) Please have your check for this amount in our office no later than 4 P.M. on [April 1]."*

**NOTE:** *By using a definite date for the alternative paragraphs, the former tenant will assume there will be legal action if it is not paid by this date, although no threat is being made.*

# Tenant Complaint—Forwarded for Action

[*Date*]

_____

_____

_____

Dear _____ :

I have received your [*letter*] relating to [*the unauthorized parking in your space*].

I have forwarded your concerns to [*the resident manager*]. [*He*] [*she*] will be contacting you directly.

I sincerely hope the problem will be solved to your satisfaction.

Yours truly,

_____

# Tenant Complaint—Action Taken

[*Date*]

_____

_____

_____

Dear _____ :

I have received your [*letter*] relating to [*unauthorized parking in your space*].

[*The offending party has been contacted*], and we hope the [*objectionable conduct will be discontinued*]. Should the problem continue, please contact me directly.

Yours truly,


_____

## Tenant Complaint—No Action Taken

[*Date*]

_____
_____
_____

Dear _____ :

I am in receipt of your complaint [*that the neighbor's children have been disturbing you. This is a family rental building, and as such the noise of children playing must be expected, although it is at times exasperating.*]

When your lease expires, we would be happy to help you find a unit that better meets your requirements.

Yours truly,

_____

**NOTE:** *As an alternative, you may wish to include this as the last sentence when the complainer has become a problem: "Because we are unable to solve your problem, we would be willing to allow you to break your lease upon _____ days' notice. Please let me know what you decide."*

# Notice to Tenant of Lessor Entry

[*Date*]

_____

_____

_____

Dear _____ :

In accordance with the terms of our lease, we will be
[*making an inspection of the premises*] [*showing the
premises to a prospective buyer*][*repairing the kitchen
floor in your unit*] at [*9 A.M.*] on [*Tuesday, February 6*].

If you are unable to be there at that time, please [*contact
this office so a more convenient time can be arranged*]
[*make certain the building manager has all necessary
keys*].

Yours truly,

_____

# Notice of Work on Premises

[*Date*]

_____

_____

_____

Dear _____ :

In the next [*few days*] [*few weeks*] we will be [*painting the lobby*] [*replacing the air conditioning*]. We hope you will not be inconvenienced by the work, which will be confined to normal working hours.

Yours truly,


_____

**NOTE:** *If access to the tenant's apartment will be necessary, the tenant should be advised.*

*You may wish to include the following paragraph: "Access will be required to your apartment on [April 15]. If you are not home, our resident manager, [Jane Smith], will remain in your unit while workers are present. [Please provide keys to the manager if required.]"*

*This letter serves another purpose, in that it serves to inform the tenants they are getting something for their rent. The owner is putting money back into the building. This serves to make a subsequent rent increase more palatable to the tenants.*

# Confirmation of Telephone Work Order

[*Date*]

_____

_____

_____

Dear _____ :

This will confirm your agreement on [*May 10*] for you to [*provide a pest control inspection*] at [*5501 Crescent Circle*]. It is understood that the work must be completed by [*June 1*].

[*Please call our office 24 hours prior to beginning work so we can be certain someone will be present to provide access to the property.*]

It is understood that your charge for said work shall be [*$125*].

Bill [*this office*] [*Mr. and Mrs. James*] for the work no later than [*July 1*].

Yours truly,

_____

**NOTE:** *If you use a work order system, continue the first paragraph with "work order number [0000] has been assigned to this project. Please reference said work order in any billing or other correspondence."*

# Chapter

# 11

# Letters to Other Brokers

# Welcome to New Broker

[*Date*]

_____
_____
_____

Dear _____ :

As a fellow real estate broker I would like to welcome you to [*the growing West Side*].

I am certain we will have many successful dealings in the coming years, since cooperation is the basis of real estate success. I will stop by to meet you personally in a few weeks after you are settled.

I wish you success in your new office and—welcome!

Sincerely,

_____

# Open House Invitation

---

**[*Clyde Realty*]**

Open House

[*922 West Broadway*]

[*Wednesday, April 5*]

[*5–8 P.M.*]

Come visit with us at our [*new office*] [*new branch office*].

Refreshments will be served

---

**NOTE:** *This flyer could also be sent to owners, investors, escrow and title companies or lenders.*

# Referral Thank-You

[*Date*]

_____

_____

_____

Dear _____ :

Thank you very much for referring [*Jane Smith*] to this office.

I have shown [*the Smiths*] a number of properties [*and I am confident I will be able to meet their housing needs*].

If ever I can be of service to you, don't hesitate to contact me.

Yours truly,

_____

**NOTE:** *If you will be splitting your commission for the referral, you could add the following to the second paragraph: "I hope I will be sending you a check within a short time."*

# Referral Thank-You—No Sale

[*Date*]

_____
_____
_____

Dear _____ :

Thank you very much for referring [*Joseph Jones*] to our office. While we contacted [*the Joneses*] promptly [*and showed them a number of homes*], they purchased a home from [*another agent*] [*a builder*].

I want you to know that our failure was not the result of lack of effort. In fact, should the opportunity again present itself, I would like to show you that [*Clyde Realty*] does make sales and is worthy of your referrals.

Yours truly,

_____

# Referral—Notice of Sale

[*Date*]

_____
_____
_____

Dear _____ :

Just a note to let you know that [*Sylvia Smith*], whom
you referred to us, has [*purchased a home through this
office*]. The closing is scheduled for [*June 1*]. On closing,
we will immediately forward your referral fee of $_____
based on our office commission of $ _____ .

We appreciate the referral and look forward to future
cooperation with your office.

Yours truly,

_____

# Referral Fee—Transmittal

[ *Date* ]

_____

_____

_____

Dear _____ :

Enclosed is our check in the amount of $ _____ , for your referral of [ *John Jones* ].

We look forward to working with you in the future.

Yours truly,

_____

Enclosures

*NOTE: Enclose check and commission statement with this letter.*

# Seeking an Investment Property

[*Date*]

_____

_____

_____

Dear _____ :

I am working with a prospective investor who has [*more than $500,000*] to invest and desires [*residential property*] [*commercial property*] [*a raw-land investment*]. My buyer's primary objective is [*appreciation*] [*income*] [*tax-sheltered income*]. [*Safety is of course a consideration as well.*]

My investor [*wants a positive cash flow*] [*will except a negative cash flow*] [*wants at least a break-even cash flow*] with an [*all-cash*] [*moderately leveraged*] [*highly leveraged*] investment.

If you have any property listed with your office that you feel would be of interest to my buyer, I would be very interested in working with you.

Yours truly,

_____

# Request for Commission or Split

[*Date*]

_____

_____

_____

Dear _____ :

[*On the morning of October 12, Mrs. Jean Jacobs of our office showed a home you have listed at 1112 Kings Drive to Mr. and Mrs. William Apple. That afternoon, you had an open house and Mr. and Mrs. William Apple stopped at the house. They told your salesperson, Jim Peters, they had seen the house that morning with Mrs. Jacobs. Mr. Peters proceeded to prepare a purchase agreement, which was signed by the Apples and accepted by the owner.*] These facts, which can be fully verified, clearly indicate that [*Clyde Realty*] is entitled to the sales commission. We therefore expect your check in the amount of [*$3,000*].

Yours truly,

_____

# Broker Commission Split Transmittal

[*Date*]

_____
_____
_____

Dear _____ :

Enclosed is our check for $ _____ , which represents_____
percent of the total commission for [*your sale*] of the
property located at [*5 Sycamore Circle*] to [*Janet
Smith*].

I have enclosed a copy of the closing statement for your
records.

Your cooperation was greatly appreciated and I look
forward to writing many more checks such as this.

Yours truly,

_____

Enclosures

# Breach of Procedure by Our Office

[*Date*]

_____
_____
_____

Dear _____ :

I want to personally apologize to you for what was an unfortunate breach of procedure by our office. [*On June 16, one of our salespersons contacted one of your owners, Janet Smith, without going through your office*]. [*One of our salespersons contacted James Smith, whose listing was in full effect with your office as to obtaining a listing.*] The reasons for the breach and the fact that at the time the salesperson did not realize [*he*] was in breach of ethics does not matter. What does matter is one of my salespersons failed to respect your rights. I want you to know I will do everything in my power to make certain such an action is not repeated.

Yours truly,

_____

# Breach of Procedure by Your Office

[*Date*]

_____

_____

_____

Dear _____ :

I am sorry to have to inform you that on [*August 21*], your salesperson [*Sylvia Smith*] [*contacted James Smith, whose listing was in full effect with our office as to obtaining a listing*].

This type of action cannot be condoned if we are to continue to engage in a profession where cooperation is the basis of our success. It is hoped that such action will not be repeated in the future.

Yours truly,

_____

# Arbitration Notice

[*Date*]

_____

_____

_____

Dear _____ :

Based on your failure to [*pay Clyde Realty the selling commission for the sale of 1112 Kings Drive to Mr. and Mrs. William Apple*], we are requesting arbitration of this matter with [*The San Marco Board of Realtors in accordance with board rules and regulations*].

Yours truly,

_____

**NOTE:** *Mandatory arbitration is only possible when both parties are members of the organization that requires arbitration.*

# Chapter

# 12

# Letters Dealing with Conflict

# Official Inquiry—Complaint

[*Date*]

_____

_____

_____

Dear _____ :

We are in receipt of your letter of [*June 3*]. I was very surprised that a complaint was made to your office. I have set forth the facts in the attachment and have included signed statements from those involved in our office.

While we believe the complaint to be entirely without merit, you can nevertheless expect our full cooperation in this matter. If you have any further questions, please do not hesitate to contact me.

Yours truly,

_____

Enclosures

# General Complaint

[*Date*]

_____

_____

_____

Dear _____ :

I am very sorry you have not been satisfied with the services of [*Clyde Realty*]. While we don't always succeed, we nevertheless strive in good faith to meet the needs of both clients and customers. Our failures are actually important, as they stimulate us to improve.

I want you to know my door is open to you at any time to openly discuss any problems, and I would be happy to meet with you at your convenience.

Your truly,

_____

# Buyer or Seller Complaint

[*Date*]

_____

_____

_____

Dear _____ :

While I am sorry to hear of your dissatisfaction with the services of one of our salespersons, I am nevertheless glad you brought this matter to my attention.

You can be assured your complaint will be fully investigated and appropriate action will be taken consistent with the circumstances. Since we serve the public and our stock in trade is really public trust, I will not tolerate even a hint of impropriety.

Yours truly,

_____

# Offer to Arbitrate

[*Date*]

_____

_____

_____

Dear _____ :

[*Clyde Realty*] would like to resolve _____ in a fair and equitable manner. What could be more fair than to submit our disagreement to an impartial arbitrator for binding arbitration? If this appears satisfactory to you, please contact me and we will work out the details of selecting an arbitrator.

[*As an alternative, in the interest of expediency we would agree to pay your company $ 3,000 for an immediate settlement.*]

Yours truly,

_____

**NOTE:** *The optional second paragraph could save you time and money. If you include it, you should be making some concession from your last position.*

# Offer of Settlement

[*Date*]

_____

_____

_____

Dear _____ :

Based on [*your letter of July 13*] [*our phone conversation on July 13*], it is clear that you feel [*Clyde Realty*] has not treated you in a fair and proper manner.

While I sincerely believe our actions were at all times fair and professional, I am nevertheless disturbed by your feelings toward us. We consider ourselves a part of the community, and want very much to maintain a harmonious relationship with all of our neighbors. Therefore, I am willing to [*reduce our fee by $ 3,000*] [*pay one-half the cost of the damaged roof*] [*remit to you one-half the March rent*].

Please let me know if my proposal meets with your approval.

Yours truly,

_____

# Notification to State about
# Violation of the Law

[*Date*]

_____

_____

_____

Dear _____ :

I am sorry to report an apparent violation of our state real estate law by [*one of my salespersons*] [*another agent*].

[*On April 12, 1989, Mr. Timothy Jones, a real estate salesperson licensed under my broker's license, accepted a $ 5,000 cash deposit from Mr. Kermit Pugh. Mr. Jones has not contacted our office since receiving the deposit and has not been home in the four days since the deposit was taken. We therefore assume Mr. Jones has appropriated the deposit to his own use. We have notified the district attorney of these facts.*]

We will fully cooperate with your office in any investigation and will promptly supply any additional information requested.

Yours truly,

_____

# Chapter

# 13

# Personnel
# Letters

# Real Estate Career Night Announcement

### Join Us for Real Estate Career Night

- Learn how many people have found new direction in their lives through real estate.

- Learn the benefits that a professional career in real estate offers:

  - The joy of helping others

  - The independence of planning your own work

  - Financial rewards directly related to your success in helping meet housing needs

  - Constant mental stimulation

If you are a retiree, a homemaker reentering the work force, a recent graduate or simply interested in a career change, this is your opportunity to learn how a real estate career meets your needs, and to ask any questions you might have.

[*Thursday, April 8th*]
[*7:00 P.M.*]
[*Clyde Realty*]
[*473 N. Main*]

[*R.S.V.P*]                    [*555-8200*]

# New or Prospective Real Estate Salesperson Solicitation

[*Date*]

_____

_____

_____

Dear _____ :

I understand you [*are currently enrolled in a real estate license preparatory course*] [*have applied to take your real estate salesperson's examination*]. I wish you success and I hope you find real estate as personally rewarding a career as many of us have.

[*Clyde Realty*] is looking for people who are sincerely seeking a career and not just a job. People who want professional growth so they can meet the needs of others; people with integrity and desire.

If you feel your goals are compatible with ours, I would like to meet with you to discuss various career options, and to let you learn about us as we learn about you.

Please call me for a personal appointment.

Sincerely,

_____

# Salesperson Solicitation—Retired

---

### Tired of Retired?

If you like people, are of good moral character and are not afraid to start a new career, I would like to hear from you.

I can offer you the personal satisfaction of helping others, a feeling of self-worth working in an independent environment, mental stimulation and financial rewards earned by your success. After a short license training program, we will work with you and guide you on your career.

Interested? Then call me today so we can meet and discuss your career in real estate.

[*Tom Flynn*]
[*General Manager*]
[*555-8200*]                              [*Clyde Realty*]

---

**NOTE:** *This flyer can be posted at retirement communities and senior centers as well as used as a mailing piece.*

# Training Session Notice

---

### Attention All Sales Personnel!

Training Session:

[*Wednesday, April 1, 9 A.M., (Prior to Caravan)*]

Subject: [*Listing Techniques*]

Attendance is mandatory unless excused by
[*Jane Jones*].

---

**NOTE:** *If there are multiple offices, the location of the session should be included.*

*If your state recognizes an independent contractor status of salespeople, you would probably not wish to make attendance mandatory, as it might jeopardize that status.*

# Sales Meeting Notice

---

### Attention: All Sales Personnel

### Sales Meeting: [*Monday, June 17, 7 A.M.*]

### [*Coffee and donuts will be served*]

### If you cannot attend for any reason, notify [*John Jones*].

---

**NOTE:** *For regular sales meetings, a form can be used with the date inserted.*

*If the firm has multiple offices, include location of meeting.*

# Notice to Salesperson of Missed Meeting

[*Date*]

_____

_____

_____

Dear _____ :

You missed the [*training session on Wednesday, April 1st, as well as the office meeting on Wednesday, April 8th.*] If you have a problem, I would be happy to provide any advice or assistance that I am capable of.

We work together in our office as a team and try to help each other. We also view training and office meetings as important functions to aid all personnel.

I want you to be part of the team and share with others your knowledge, experience and support. I look forward to your attendance and support in the future.

Sincerely,


_____


**NOTE:** *Personnel matters should be handled personally rather than by letter whenever possible.*

# Notice to Salesperson—Unauthorized Absence

[*Date*]

_____

_____

_____

Dear _____ :

On [*Wednesday, March 1*], you were scheduled for [*floor time*] [*open house at 111 Circle Drive*]. You were not present and I was not notified you would be absent so other arrangements could be made.

When a salesperson misses [*floor time, we have inadequate coverage of our calls. This results in a waste of advertising dollars and lost opportunities*] [*an open house not only can we waste advertising dollars, we can have angry owners and angrier potential buyers who have made a trip to see a home that is not open*].

While I realize there are legitimate emergencies, nevertheless it is imperative that the office be notified of any absence when you are scheduled to be present.

Yours truly,

_____

**NOTE:** *A personal meeting would be the preferred way to handle a matter such as this.*

# Problem Notification

[*Date*]

_____

_____

_____

Dear _____ :

I am sorry to say I have received a complaint about

_____ .

[*Could you please meet with me*] [*Could you please meet with me and our attorney*] on [*Friday, April 12 at 4 P.M.*] at [*5 Crescent Boulevard, Suite 1800*]?

[*I have arranged a meeting between Mr. Jones, you and myself at our office at 4 P.M. on Thursday, April 12. If you could come at 3 P.M., it will give me a chance to get all of the facts straight.*]

Yours truly,

_____

# Commission Dispute or Hearing

[*Date*]

_____

_____

_____

Dear _____ :

I would like you and _____ to meet with me in my office on [*April 1*], at [*4 P.M.*], for the purpose of resolving the disagreement as to the entitlement to [*listing*][*sales*] commission for the [*listing of*][*sale of*][*111 West Jackson Street*].

Sincerely,

_____

# Office Dispute Decision

[*Date*]

_____

_____

_____

Dear _____ :

In accordance with your employment contract with
[*Clyde Realty*], commission disputes within the office
shall be resolved by binding broker arbitration.

On [*April 11*], I heard your claim for [*one-half of the sale
commission for the sale of the property at 111 West
Jackson Street, as well as the claim of Emily Jones for
the entire sales commission*].

My decision in this case is that [*Emily Jones is entitled
to the entire sales commission for the sale of 111 West
Jackson Street*].

Sincerely,

**NOTE:** *This letter can only be used if the salesperson's contract
calls for binding arbitration by the broker.*

# Salesperson Award

[*Date*]

_____
_____
_____

Dear _____ :

This is to inform you that [*Jerry Jones*] is the grand winner of [*salesman of the month for January*]. This award was achieved with [*sales of $2,851,000*].

The reward of [*a three-day Las Vegas holiday for two*] can be claimed at [*Anderson Travel*].

Our warmest congratulations,

_____

**NOTE:** *Awards should generally be made before the entire sales force. If a notice is used, the notice should be by telegram or special delivery letter.*

# Happy Birthday #1

[*Date*]

_____
_____
_____

Dear _____ :

Well, another year has past. In retrospect, it has been
a good year for you. You are respected by your fellow
workers as a knowledgeable and caring person. You are
dedicated and have taken the reins of your own destiny.
Most important, we regard you as our friend.

A very happy birthday, [*Martin*], from all of us.

_____          _____

_____          _____

_____          _____

**NOTE:** *A letter is a warmer approach than just a card.*

# Happy Birthday #2

**Happy Birthday, [*Clarence*]**

We all wish you the very best
on your birthday

Good Health
Good Friends
A Happy Family
Prosperity

We hope you are with us at [*Clyde Realty*] to celebrate
a great many more of them.

Again—A very happy birthday!

\_\_\_\_\_                                    \_\_\_\_\_

\_\_\_\_\_                                    \_\_\_\_\_

\_\_\_\_\_                                    \_\_\_\_\_

# Wedding Anniversary

[*Date*]

_____

_____

_____

Dear _____ :

My very best wishes to both of you on your wedding anniversary. As a small token of my personal regard for you, I have enclosed [ *a certificate for dinner for two at the Golden Palm* ].

It is my sincere hope that you have a joyful celebration of this and many more anniversaries.

Yours truly,


_____


**NOTE:** *Include the Husband's and Wife's names in the salutation.*

# Employee Anniversary with Firm

[*Date*]

_____

_____

_____

Dear _____ :

I don't know if you noticed, but it's our anniversary. On
[*June 1*], it will have been [*five*] years since you joined
[*Clyde Realty*]. It has been a time filled with many
successes and a lot of hard work. During this time you
have helped to make possible the dream of home ownership for many families.

I want you to realize your efforts have not gone unnoticed
or unappreciated. I am proud to have you with the firm
and look forward to a great many more anniversaries.

Sincerely,

_____

# Birth of Son or Daughter

[*Date*]

_____

_____

_____

Dear _____ :

My warmest congratulations on the birth of your [*daughter*] [*son*]. Little [*Mary Elizabeth*] [*John Martin*] has a [*father*] [*mother*] [*she*] [*he*] can be proud of.

This small gift is but a token of my regard for you and the joy I share with you on this miraculous event.

Yours truly,

_____

# Death in Agent's Family

[*Date*]

_____

_____

_____

Dear _____ :

I would like to offer my sincere condolences to you [*and your son*] on your recent loss. I know how much you thought of [*Mary Jane*] and can understand your feelings at this time.

[*Mary Jane*] brought joy to the lives of her family and friends, and her memory will live on in those whose lives [*she*] influenced.

Thinking of you,


_____


**NOTE:** *This personal note is in addition to flowers sent for the funeral.*

# Death of Salesperson or Associate

[*Date*]

_____

_____

_____

Dear _____ :

I wish to offer my personal condolences to you. [*Mary*]
[*Henry*] was [*an associate broker*] [*salesperson*] with
[*Clyde Realty*] for [*7 years*], [*all too short a time*]. [*She*]
[*He*] was liked and respected by all of us as well as the
many clients [*she*] [*he*] helped in meeting their real
estate needs. [*Mary*] [*Henry*] gave unsparingly of [*her-
self*] [*himself*] in helping others.

I share in your feeling of loss and want you to know
[*Mary*] [*Henry*] will be truly missed.

_____

**NOTE:** *This letter would be sent to a spouse or parent upon the
death of an agent.*

# Letter of Recommendation

[*Date*]

_____

_____

_____

Dear _____ :

[*Janet Jones*] worked for [*Clyde Realty*] from [*August 1978*] to [*June 1990*] as a real estate sales associate. [*Janet*] always exhibited the utmost integrity and a sincere desire to help others in meeting their housing needs.

[*I would hire Janet Jones again without hesitation.*]

Yours truly,


_____

# Notice to Employee—Termination

[*Date*]

_____

_____

_____

Dear _____ :

I am very sorry to inform you that we are unable to retain you as a [*sales associate*] with [*Clyde Realty*]. [*I have enclosed your real estate license.*] [*Your contract rights as to sales and listings in progress will be strictly honored by our office.*] [*It would be appreciated if you will send me your office keys.*]

I wish you success in any future endeavors, and if there is any way I can be of help to you or if you have any questions, please contact me personally.

Sincerely,

_____

**NOTE:** *Normally, this should be handled in a face-to-face meeting. Avoid criticism or any accusations as to honesty as it could be construed as libel.*

# Chapter

# 14

# Lender, Attorney and Escrow Letters

# Request for Loan Terms—General

[*Date*]

_____

_____

_____

Dear _____ :

Please supply me with your current loan requirements and terms for fixed-rate and adjustable rate mortgages.

I would also appreciate receiving several loan application packages.

Yours truly,


_____

# Request for Loan Terms—Specific Buyer

[*Date*]

_____

_____

_____

Dear _____ :

Please supply me with your current loan terms for a
[*fixed-rate 30-year amortized loan*] [*25-year adjustable
rate mortgage*] [*for a home in Middlebury Heights. The
purchase price is $ 130,000, and the buyer has a $ 30,000
down payment.*]

It would be appreciated if you would also include several
loan applications.

Yours truly,

_____

# Loan Application Transmittal

[*Date*]

_____
_____
_____

Dear _____ :

Enclosed you will find the completed loan application of [*John and Mary Brown*] for the purchase of a home located at [*65 Jupiter Lane*].

If you have any problems whatsoever, or desire any additional information, please contact _____ or me.

Your truly,


_____

Enclosure

# Request to Lender to Expedite Loan Request

[*Date*]

_____

_____

_____

Dear _____ :

[*Mr. and Mrs. Smith*] recently applied for a loan through your office for the purchase of the home at [*111 Stardust Circle*].

Because of unusual needs of the seller it is necessary that this sale be closed by [*August 1, 1990*]. While I realize this places a strain on your office, I would nevertheless greatly appreciate any efforts you can provide to expedite this transaction.

Yours truly,


_____


**NOTE:** *When time is important, regular calls to check on status should be made.*

# Request for Abstract Update

[*Date*]

_____

_____

_____

Dear _____ :

Please update the enclosed abstract on the following described property: [*insert legal description*].

Please bill _____ for this service.

Yours truly,


_____

Enclosure

# Thank-You to Loan Officer #1

[Date]

_____

_____

_____

Dear _____ :

I would like to personally thank you for your help in arranging the financing for [Sherman and Joyce Mack] on their recent home purchase at [72 Lynn Court].

You not only delivered the loan in a timely manner, but you provided counseling services as well, which was greatly appreciated. You made what is ordinarily a difficult process a pleasant experience. I hope to have many future loans with you and your firm.

Yours truly,

_____

cc: [Jane Smith, President, ABC Savings and Loan]

**NOTE:** _A letter such as this, with copies to the president of the lending bank, S & L or loan company, will be appreciated by the loan officer. You can expect any future loan problems to be treated by this loan officer as a priority item._

# Thank-You to Loan Officer #2

[*Date*]

_____

_____

_____

Dear _____ :

I want to personally thank you for your herculean efforts that resulted in our being able to close the [*James C. Smith*] loan by [*August 1st*].

Your attention to detail coupled with your honest, straightforward approach proved what others said couldn't be done can be accomplished with a positive, "can-do" attitude. It was a pleasure working with you and I look forward to many further transactions through your firm.

Yours truly,

_____

cc: [*John Jones, President, ABC Savings and Loan*]

**NOTE:** *This letter and its copy will give you a future ally in the lender's office.*

# Request for Loan Payoff Balance

[*Date*]

_____

_____

_____

Dear _____ :

Please provide the payoff balance for loan no. [*00190356*] in the name of [Janet Smith], based on a payoff date of [*January 1, 1999*].

Yours truly,

_____

# Request for List of Repossessions

[*Date*]

_____
_____
_____

Dear _____ :

Please provide a list of your present repossessions and information as to:

1. Address and size
2. Price and terms (if applicable)
3. Obtaining keys for showings (is a master key available?).

Yours truly,

_____

# Request for Attorney Title Opinion

[*Date*]

_____

_____

_____

Dear _____ :

Please provide a title opinion for [*Mr. and Mrs. Thomas Wooley*] for the purchase of [*insert legal descriptions*].

The updated abstract is enclosed.

Please send the opinion and the abstract to [*my office*]. Your invoice should be [*made out to Mr. and Mrs. Thomas Wolley, but sent to me*].

Yours truly,

_____

Enclosure

# Purchase Contract for Attorney Approval

[*Date*]

_____

_____

_____

Dear _____ :

Enclosed is the completed purchase contract for the purchase by [*Jim and Jane Schmidt*] of [*111 Crescent Cove*]. If after your review you determine that the agreement is legally sufficient, please have [*Mr. and Mrs. Schmidt*] sign and return [*three*] copies to this office.

Yours truly,

_____

Enclosure

**NOTE:** *Don't mention changes or modifications. Most attorneys will do so without your reminder.*

# Thank-You Letter to Attorney

[*Date*]

_____

_____

_____

Dear _____ :

It was a pleasure working with you on the [*Smiths'*] [*sale*] [*purchase*]. Your professional and helpful manner made what is often a confrontation a friendly and beneficial transaction.

If ever I am asked to recommend a real estate attorney, I will not hesitate to provide your name.

Yours truly,

_____

**NOTE:** *A thank-you letter such as this will allow you to deal with the attorney in a more relaxed manner in the future.*

# Request for Escrow Fee and Cost Schedules

[*Date*]

_____

_____

_____

Dear _____ :

Please supply me with your current escrow fee schedule as well as your schedule of escrow costs.

Yours truly,

_____

# Request for Private Mortgage Insurance Information

[*Date*]

_____

_____

_____

Dear _____ :

Please send me information as to your requirements for and costs of private mortgage insurance. Please also include several application packages.

Yours truly,


_____

# Inquiry about Escrow Status for Closing

[*Date*]

_____

_____

_____

Dear _____ :

Please provide me with the present status of the escrow for closing [*111 West Jackson Street*], [*Hirt-sellers/ Scallon-buyers*].

If there is any problem that could prevent a [*June 1*] closing please contact me at once.

Yours truly,


_____

# Chapter

# 15

# Press Releases

# New Owner

## [Retired Banker Chooses Meadowbrook]

Mr. and Mrs. [*Angus McCook*] have recently purchased [*a new home on Clancy Lane in Meadowbrook*]. [*Mr. McCook was active in banking for 40 years, having started as a teller with the Midvale Bank and rising to the presidency of the Newport Banking Group, one of the largest bank holding companies in the state.*]

[*Mr. and Mrs. McCook*] indicated they were attracted to Meadowbrook because of the [*choice of several outstanding golf courses and the general country atmosphere, close to the amenities of urban life*]. The purchase was arranged through the [*Meadowbrook office of Clyde Realty*].

**NOTE:** *A press release on a buyer is appropriate when the buyer has a distinguished or interesting background. Photos with captions should be included.*

# Sale and Purchase

### [Smith Building Sold]

[Jim Anderson] of [Clyde Realty] recently sold [the Smith Building] at [5 Commercial Avenue]. The former owners, [Alice and Gertrude Smith], owned this landmark property for [45] years.

The purchasers, [Mr. and Mrs. Thomas Blake] of [San Juno] have indicated they will [extensively remodel the property] [move their offices to the property]. [Mr. Blake is president of Blake Motors in Covina.]

[This sale brings the first quarter sales of Clyde Realty to over $17,000,000, which is an increase of 16 percent from last year. Mr. Joseph Clyde, vice president of sales, has indicated the interest in large commercial properties such as the Smith Building has increased significantly, and he predicts continued sales increases for the foreseeable future.]

# Ground Breaking

### New Project—[*Woodlake Village*]

[*Wilson Developers*] held their official ground breaking for the new [*122 single-family home Woodlake Village development*] on [*Wednesday, March 1st*]. Located [*on the northwest corner of Dunn Road and Woodlake Parkway*], the [*three-and four-bedroom family homes*] will feature [*up to 2,400 square feet. All homes will have three-car garages, tile roofs and eurostyle kitchens*].

[*Peggy Wilson*], the project sales coordinator for [*Clyde Realty*], the exclusive sales agent for [*Woodlake Village*], has indicated that the choice location coupled with moderate prices, starting at [*$122,500*] with [*10 percent*] financing, has already created an exceptional word-of-mouth interest in the development. According to [*Peggy Wilson*], the early reservations have been primarily from professionals in the real estate and construction industries.

*NOTE: For ground-breaking ceremonies, consider including a captioned photograph with local civic leaders and a builder representative as well as an agent of your firm.*

# Subdivision Opening

### Grand Opening—[*Woodlake Village*]

The grand opening of [*Wilson Development's*] new [*Woodlake Village*] is scheduled for [*Saturday and Sunday, June 5th and 6th*]. Located [*on the northwest corner of Dunn Road and Woodlake Parkway*], the development features [*three- and four-bedroom family homes starting at $122,500, with 10 percent financing available*]. All homes include [*three-car garages, tile roofs, and eurostyle kitchens*].

[*Peggy Wilson*] the [*sales coordinator*] for [*Clyde Realty*], which is the exclusive sales agent for the project, has indicated exceptional interest has developed in [*Woodlake Village*] due to the [*choice location and moderate pricing policy*].

According to [*Mrs. Wilson*], [*the grand opening will feature six decorator furnished models and there will be refreshments and gifts for opening day visitors*].

**NOTE:** *You might want to include a photo or artist's rendering of one of the models.*

# First Sale in Subdivision

---

### First Sale Made at [*English Village*]

[*Clyde Realty*], the exclusive sales agent for [*English Village*], has announced that [*Dr. and Mrs. Timothy Marks*] are the first home purchasers in [*the exclusive enclave of 16 estate homes in Bellwood*].

The [*Marks*] chose a [*3,600 square foot English country design*]. According to [*Dr. Marks*], they decided on [*English Village*] because of [*the huge lots, views, quality of design and construction as well as the country ambiance, which is so important with four small children*].

[*Currently three of the estate homes are under construction with the Marks' home scheduled for completion by August.*]

---

**NOTE:** *For a press release that provides information about a purchaser, be certain to obtain permission from the purchaser.*

*In addition to publicity about your firm, a press release such as this one significantly reduces the possibility the purchaser will attempt to avoid the purchase closing.*

# Milestone Sale in Subdivision

### [*100th Sale Announced for Orchard Heights*]

[*Henry Ammenson*], [*project director*] for [*Clyde Realty*], has announced that the [*100th new home in Orchard Heights has been sold since November*]. According to [*Mr. Ammenson*], this has been one of the most successful subdivisions in the area because of the tremendous value offered in housing at a premier location. The problem has been not being able to build the homes fast enough. [*Mr. Ammenson indicates that at the present sales rate, the entire subdivision will be sold out by June 1st.*]

# New Office Opening

### [*Clyde Realty Opens Newhall Office*]

[*Clyde Realty*] has announced the opening of a, [*fourth*] office [*in the Jenkins Center, at 922 West 60th Street in Newhall*]. According to [*Oscar Brown*], manager of the new office, the expansion was necessary to fulfill the growing needs of [*the West Valley*]. While the office will specialize in residential sales, the services will also include [*investment sales and property management*]. [*The new office will also coordinate the sales of several new subdivisions in the area.*] [*Clyde Realty*], currently has [*more than 60 salespersons with total sales last year exceeding $100,000,000 making the firm one of the fastest growing brokerage offices in the county*].

# New Associate or Salesperson

---

### [*Henry Gibbs*] joins [*Clyde Realty*]

[*Thomas Flynn*], [*General Manager*] of [*Clyde Realty*], announced that [*Mr. Henry Gibbs*] recently joined the firm as a [*sales associate*] [*associate broker*]. [*Mr. Gibbs*] will be involved with [*home sales, primarily in the West Valley*].

[*Mrs. Gibbs*] is [*a graduate of Syracuse University and spent 12 years as a food broker in Chicago*]. [*He*] obtained [*his*] real estate license [*two years ago, and was previously associated with Boniface Construction Company, selling new homes in the Bellwood Heights development*]. [*Mr. Gibbs is a member of Thunderbird Country Club and resides in Bellwood Heights with his wife Eileen and their two daughters.*]

---

**NOTE:** *Send photo with all personnel press releases.*

# Promotion or Appointment

## New [*Sales Manager*]

[*Henry Clyde, President of Clyde Realty*] has announced that [*Janet Jones*] has been appointed [*sales manager*] of [*Clyde Realty*].

[*Ms. Jones*] brings a wealth of experience to the position. [*She*] was formerly associated with [*Smith Realty*] as [*assistant sales manager*]. [*Ms. Jones*] has had more that [*eight*] years' experience in [*sales*] [*real estate sales*]. [*Ms. Jones*] has been with [*Clyde Realty*] for [*four years*]. [*Ms. Jones has received numerous honors, including membership in the prestigious Clyde Realty Million Dollar Roundtable.*] [*Ms. Jones received her bachelor's degree in business from Yale University.*] [*Ms. Jones attended New York University.*] [*She*] lives with [*her*] family in [*Midvale Heights*]. [*She has two children, John, nine years old, and Tammy, six.*] [*Her husband*] [*teaches English at South High School*]. [*Ms. Jones*] is active in [*Soroptimists and is an assistant girl scout leader*].

# Sales Award

---

### Salesperson of the (Month) (Year)

[*Joseph Evans*], [*Sales Manager*] of [*Clyde Realty*], has announced that [*Patricia Jones*] has been named [*sales associate of the [month] [year.]*]

During the [*month*] [*past year*], [*Ms. Jones*] has [*sold*] [*listed*] [*more than $3 million in real estate*] [*19 properties*]. [*Ms. Jones*] has been associated with [*Clyde Realty*] [*since 1983*] [*for seven years*]. Prior to joining [*Clyde Realty*], [*she*] was [*a professor of zoology at Western State University*]. [*Mrs. Jones lives in Middletown with her husband and four children.*]

---

# Sale of Real Estate Firm

### New Owner Announced for [*Clyde Realty*]

[*Clyde Realty*] has announced the firm has been sold [*by its founder, Angus Clyde, to the firm's General Manager, Thomas Flynn. Angus Clyde founded Clyde Realty in 1947, and it was the oldest real estate firm in the county under the same ownership*].

[*Clyde Realty*] currently has [*62 salespersons operating from their offices at 922 West Broadway*]. [*Angus Clyde*] estimates that over the years, the firm has sold over [*25,000*] properties, with sales [*in the hundreds of millions of dollars*].

[*Thomas Flynn*] has been associated with [*Clyde Realty*] [*for 11 years, starting as a salesperson and the last four years, as General Manager*]. [*Mr. Flynn who is a business graduate of Michigan State University, indicates that the philosophy and policies of Angus Clyde will continue, as will the firm's name.*]

**NOTE:** *Photographs should be included, especially of Mr. Flynn.*

# Chapter
# 16

# Miscellaneous Letters

# Transmittal Letter to Newspaper of Ad Copy

[*Date*]

_____

_____

_____

Dear _____ :

I wish the following to run [*from* _____ *to* _____ ]
in the classified section under the categories indicated:

    Category [_____ ]

    _____

    _____

    _____

    Category [_____ ]

    _____

    _____

    _____

    _____

    Please bill these ads to my account.

[*Thomas Flynn*]
[*Clyde Realty*]

**NOTE:** *Give any instructions as to type style or size of type, if*
*applicable.*

# Notice to Newspaper of Mistake in Advertisement

[*Date*]

_____

_____

_____

Attention: Classified Advertisement Department Editor

On [_____ ] we placed an ad to read as follows:

[_____

_____

_____ ]

Due to an apparent typesetting error, the ad appeared on [_____ ] as follows:

[_____

_____ ]

Because of the error, [*the effectiveness of the ad was materially diminished*] [*the ad was of no benefit to our firm*]. We therefore expect [*an appropriate adjustment because of your error*] [*the ad charge to be fully credited on our next billing*] [*the ad to be reproduced as placed on _____ without charge*].

Yours truly,

_____

**NOTE:** *You may wish to use a yellow "highlighter" to indicate the error.*

# Charity Ticket Response

[*Date*]

_____

_____

_____

Dear _____ :

Enclosed is our check for $ _____ for [*two*] tickets.
The remainder of the tickets are enclosed.

We are always happy to provide assistance to local
organizations.

We wish you good luck on your event.

Yours truly,


_____



**NOTE:** *Charities generally send out books of tickets. This is a*
*positive response without buying all of the tickets.*

# Thank You for Referring Your Friend

[*Date*]

_____

_____

_____

Dear _____ :

I want to thank you for referring your friend [*John Jones*] to our office.

It is referrals such as yours that let us know we are doing a good job in meeting the real estate needs of our neighbors.

I [*am working with Mr. and Mrs. Jones to find them a new home*] [*was successful in finding a lovely new home for Mr. and Mrs. Jones*] [*was able to find a buyer for their lovely home*] [*feel certain I will be able to find a buyer for their lovely home*].

I want you to know that any future referrals will be appreciated and I will strive to meet the needs of your friends.

Yours truly,

_____

# INDEX